Services Sector in India

Recent Policy Initiatives

Services Sector in India

Recent Policy Initiatives

A. Vijayakumar

NEW NC CENTURY
New Century Publications
New Delhi, India

New Century Publications
4800/24, Bharat Ram Road,
Ansari Road, Daryaganj,
New Delhi -110 002 (India)

Tel.: 011 – 2324 7798, 4358 7398, 6539 6605
Fax: 011 – 4101 7798
E-mail: indiatax@vsnl.com
www.newcenturypublications.com

Editorial office:
34, Gujranwala Town, Part-2,
Delhi - 110 009

Tel.: 27247805, 27464774

First Published – **September 2008**

ISBN: 978-81-7708-189-3

Published by New Century Publications and printed at Salasar Imaging Systems, New Delhi

Designs: Patch Creative Unit, New Delhi

PRINTED IN INDIA

THE BOOK

Since the early 1990s, the growth process in India has been marked by a remarkable performance of services sector. The experience of developed countries suggests that growth of services sector followed the growth of industrial sector. However, India's experience in this regard is somewhat different. The sectoral shift in favour of services sector over the last two decades has taken place in the face of an almost stagnant share of industry and a reduced share of agriculture in GDP. In fact, it was the growth performance of the services sector during the 1990s which sustained the overall growth of the Indian economy, particularly in times of adverse agricultural shocks and industrial slowdown.

While software exports are a well-known success story, India is now an important venue for many tasks in services such as financial accounting, call centres, processing insurance claims, and medical transcription. The future potential of growth in these areas appears to be considerable.

This book explains recent policy measures by the Government of India to make India's services sector internationally competitive. The book focuses on the following services: financial services, IT and IT-enabled services, retail trading services, healthcare services, insurance services, educational services, transport and communication services, and tourism. It also includes a chapter on taxation of services in India.

THE AUTHOR

Dr. A. Vijayakumar is a Reader in the Faculty of Commerce, Erode Arts College, Erode. He obtained his M.Phil. and Ph.D. degrees from Bharathiar University in 1990 and 1997 respectively. He has published 80 research papers and articles in national and international journals. He has successfully completed a number of research projects funded by University Grants Commission (UGC), New Delhi and Indian Council of Social Science Research (ICSSR), New Delhi. Dr. Vijayakumar specializes in cost and management accounting and research methodology.

PREFACE

The services sector has been the key driver of growth of the Indian economy since the initiation of economic reforms in the early 1990s. Although the growth of the Indian services sector has been broad-based, certain infrastructure services such as communications and insurance and banking have grown more rapidly, underpinning growth of the services sector as a whole. India has emerged as one of the leading exporters of commercial services in the world.

India is now Asia's third largest economy and has the world's fourth largest foreign exchange reserves. Technology, competition, and benchmarking to the best international practices are the driving force of India's development efforts. The country is making rapid strides in all these areas. Technology is getting upgraded rapidly and competition in the market place has become fierce. The vibrant IT industry is contributing immensely by providing information about latest technology and international business practices.

The experience of developed countries suggests that growth of services sector followed the growth of industrial sector. However, India's experience in this regard is somewhat different. The sectoral shift in favour of services sector over the last two decades has taken place in the face of an almost stagnant share of industry and a reduced share of agriculture in GDP. In fact, it was the growth performance of the services sector during the 1990s which sustained the overall growth of the Indian economy, particularly in times of adverse agricultural shocks and industrial slowdown.

The robust performance of the services sector is attributable to a host of factors, internal and external, the following among which are more important.

1. Liberalization of the financial sector acted as a catalyst for faster growth of the financial services.
2. Industrial sector reforms provided the appropriate

environment for increased demand for producer services.
3. Reforms in infrastructure services also contributed to the growth of services sector.
4. Services sector also benefited from external demand, the typical example of which is the software industry.

While software exports are a well-known success story, India is now an important venue for many tasks in services such as financial accounting, call centres, processing insurance claims, and medical transcription. The future potential of growth in these areas appears to be considerable.

The quality of physical infrastructure and infrastructural services is crucial for the competitiveness of the services sector, although the importance of individual elements of infrastructure differs from sub-sector to sub-sector. Telecommunications, power, roads, railways, ports, airports are all important for the efficiency of the services sector. The telecommunications sector in India stands apart as it can be said to have reached world standards. However, there are serious shortcomings in all other areas resulting in high logistics cost for service enterprises.

An effort has been made in this book to capture recent developments in the services sector of the Indian economy.

A. Vijayakumar

CONTENTS

1

Growth of Services Sector in India

1.1 Recent Trends in the Composition of India's Gross Domestic Product (GDP)

The composition of GDP in India has undergone significant changes since 1980, and particularly after the launching of economic reforms in early 1990s. The relative share of agriculture in GDP which stood at 38.1 per cent in 1980-81, declined to 30.9 per cent in 1990-91, 26.8 per cent in 1998-99 and was recorded at 19.7 per cent for the year 2005-06. Conversely, the share of services increased from 41.0 per cent in 1980-81 to 43.7 per cent in 1990-91 and 60.9 per cent in 2005-06. The share of industry in GDP moved up from 20.9 per cent in 1980-81 to 28.4 per cent in 1990-91 but then declined gradually to stand at 19.5 per cent in 2005-06 (Table 1.1).

The compositional shift in favour of the service sector, brought about by the rapid expansion of the service sector, is in line with the development experience of a number of countries. It is well-known that as an economy develops, the shares of industrial and service sectors in GDP increase at the cost of the agricultural sector.

1.2 Importance of Services Sector in the Indian Economy

The services sector has been the key driver of growth of the Indian economy in the past decade, during which India has ranked among ten fastest growing economies in the world, with average economic growth at over 7 per cent a year, and over 8.5 per cent in the last four years. During the 1990s, India's services sector grew at an average annual rate of 9 per cent, well ahead of the growth rate of industry at 5.8 per cent per annum and that of agriculture at 3.1 per cent per annum. At present services account for about 26 per cent of total organized sector employment in the country.

Table 1.1: Changes in Inter-sectoral Composition of GDP in India: Selected Years (per cent)

Year	Share in GDP		
	Agriculture	Industry	Services
1980-81	38.1	20.9	41.0
1984-85	35.9	22.9	41.1
1990-91	30.9	28.4	43.7
1995-96	26.0	26.7	47.0
1996-97	28.0	22.0	49.9
1997-98	26.4	22.3	51.2
1998-99	26.8	22.0	51.2
2001-02	24.4	19.3	56.3
2002-03	21.9	19.9	58.3
2003-04	22.2	19.5	58.3
2004-05	20.8	19.5	59.7
2005-06*	19.7	19.5	60.9

*Advance estimates.

Source: Reserve Bank of India, *Report on Currency and Finance*, 1998-99, p. V-6; *Report on Currency and Finance*, 2004-05, p.6.

Although the growth of the Indian services sector has been broad-based, certain infrastructure services such as communications and insurance and banking have grown more rapidly, underpinning growth of the services sector as a whole.

India has emerged as one of the leading exporters of commercial services in the world. In recent years, India's merchandise exports to the rest of the world crossed the 1 per cent mark, growing at an average 25 per cent over the last 3 years, but the net merchandise trade balance is negative. However, India's invisible (net) inflows continue to compensate the growing trade deficit to a large extent. In

2005-06, India's commercial services exports constituted around 37 per cent of the country's global exports (goods and services). Indian exports of commercial services have been among the fastest growing globally in the past 15 years.

1.3 Economic Reforms and Services Sector

After the reforms initiated in 1991, the Indian economy has been growing faster than its historical growth rate. The Indian economy responded to the economic reforms of the 1990s with a higher growth performance than in previous decades. The economy, therefore, has shown that it is capable of achieving high growth rates in response to the implementation of appropriate economic reform policies.

India is now Asia's third largest economy and has the world's fourth largest foreign exchange reserves. Technology, competition, and benchmarking to the best international practices have to be the driving force of India's development efforts. The country is making rapid strides in all these areas. Technology is getting upgraded rapidly and competition in the market place has become fierce. The vibrant IT industry is contributing immensely by providing information about latest technology and international business practices.

With quantitative restrictions on imports removed, customs duties progressively lowered, and foreign investment, both direct and portfolio, liberalized, integration of India into the global economy is progressing fast. Buoyant export performance, a surplus in the current account, and the strong balance of payments position demonstrate the success of the country in this integration process.

When the Indian economy was opened to external competition in the early 1990s, many feared decline of domestic companies which had enjoyed protection through high tariff and non-tariff walls for about half a century since Independence. These fears were true but short-lived. After facing global competition for about a decade, Indian industry is emerging much stronger to find its rightful place not only in the domestic market, but also in foreign lands.

Since the 1980s, the growth process in India has been marked by a remarkable performance of services sector. The experience of developed countries suggests that growth of services sector followed the growth of industrial sector. However, India's experience in this regard is somewhat different. The sectoral shift in favour of services sector over the last two decades has taken place in the face of an almost stagnant share of industry and a reduced share of agriculture in GDP. In fact, it was the growth performance of the services sector during the 1990s which sustained the overall growth of the Indian economy, particularly in times of adverse agricultural shocks and industrial slowdown.

The robust performance of the services sector is attributable to a host of factors, internal and external, the following among which are more important.

1. Liberalization of the financial sector acted as a catalyst for faster growth of the financial services.
2. Industrial sector reforms provided the appropriate environment for increased demand for producer services.
3. Reforms in infrastructure services also contributed to the growth of services sector.
4. Services sector also benefited from external demand, the typical example of which is the software industry.

While software exports are a well-known success story, India is now an important venue for many tasks in services such as financial accounting, call centres, processing insurance claims, and medical transcription. The future potential of growth in these areas appears to be considerable.

1.4 Infrastructure Bottlenecks

The quality of physical infrastructure and infrastructural services is crucial for the competitiveness of the services sector, although the importance of individual elements of infrastructure differs from sub-sector to sub-sector. Telecommunications, power, roads, railways, ports, airports are all important for the efficiency of the services sector. The telecommunications sector in India stands apart as it can be said to have reached world standards. However, there are serious shortcomings in all other areas resulting in high logistics cost for service enterprises.

The power situation in the country has remained bad with deficiencies in both quality and quantity of electricity supplies. Supplies have been increasing but they have been outstripped by demand with the result that shortfall between peak demand and availability has increased in the past few years. Maintaining captive power generation units increases the costs of hotels, hospitals, retail outlets, banks and IT and ITES establishments.

A massive National Highways Development Programme is underway but the stretches not taken up for development are in a state of disrepair. The State highways are being maintained well in some States but in others their condition is deplorable. For efficiency and for cutting down the logistic costs the entire road network needs to be maintained in good condition. Another big impediment is the stoppage of vehicles at the check-posts at inter-state borders by commercial taxes, transport, forest and police officials even if the vehicles are merely transiting through the States. The cumulative result of all this is that even if the road surface is good and has adequate width, vehicles move at a slow speed.

Indian Railways have been performing well in recent years and the involvement of private operators for the transportation of containers has increased the efficiency of movement of goods by train. However, the goods trains are still being slowed down by congestion in saturated corridors like Delhi-Mumbai. The Dedicated Freight Corridors on the Western and Eastern routes have been on the anvil for the last two years but there has been no perceptible progress in their implementation.

1.5 Role of the Government in the Changed Scenario

The process of liberalisation, privatisation and globalisation has a bearing on the economic role of Central and

State Governments in India. In the context of this redefined role, the Tenth Five Year Plan (2002-07) observed, "It is now generally recognized that government in the past tended to take on too many responsibilities, imposing severe strains on its limited financial and administrative capabilities and also stifling individual initiative...This is not to say that government has no role to play, or only a minimalist role, in promoting development. On the contrary, Government has a very important role indeed, but a different one from that envisaged in the past. There are many areas, e.g. the social sectors, where its role will clearly have to expand. There are other areas, e.g. infrastructure development, where gaps are large and the private sector cannot be expected to step in significantly. In these areas, the role of Government may have to be expanded and restructured. It will have to expand in some areas of infrastructure development which are unlikely to attract private investment, e.g. rural infrastructure and road development. In others, e.g. telecommunications, power, ports, etc., the private sector can play a much greater role, provided an appropriate policy frame-work is in place. Here, the role of the Government needs to change to facilitate such investment as much as possible while still remaining a public sector service provider for quite some time. In all these areas, the role of the government as a regulator ensuring a fair deal for consumers, transparency and accountability, and a level playing field is also extremely important." [1] The process of economic reforms in India initiated in 1991 seems irreversible. There is enough evidence that Government is withdrawing, though gradually, as a controller and licenser of private activity and allowing competition and market forces to guide investment decisions.

Note

1. Government of India, Planning Commission, Tenth Five Year Plan (2002-07), Vol. I, pp. 7-8.

2

Financial Services

Until the early 1990s, the role of the financial system in India was primarily restricted to the function of channeling resources from surplus to deficit sectors. Whereas the financial system performed this role reasonably well, its operations came to be marked by some serious deficiencies over the years. The Indian Government determined the quantum, allocation and the price of credit, a situation referred to as *financial repression* [1] by some experts.

It was in this backdrop, that wide-ranging financial sector reforms in India were introduced as an integral part of the economic reforms initiated in the early 1990s.

2.1 Financial Repression to Financial Liberalization (1991 onward)

Considering the strategic importance of the financial sector, the Government of India set up a Committee on Financial System in 1991 under the chairmanship of Mr. M. Narasimham. It was asked to examine all aspects relating to the structure, organisation, functions and procedures of the Indian financial system. The Committee submitted its report in November 1991. It was presented to Parliament in December 1991.

Financial sector reforms during the last decade and a half have focused on the following.

- Elimination of segmentation across various markets in order to facilitate transmission of impulses across markets.
- Easing the liquidity management process.
- Making resource allocation more efficient across the economy.

For this purpose, restrictions on pricing of assets have

been removed, new instruments have been introduced, and technological infrastructure has been strengthened. In short, liberalization of the financial sector has included, among others, the following.

- Deregulation of interest rates.
- Introduction of new products.
- Relaxation in investment norms for financial intermediaries, especially banks.
- Lowering of restrictions on specialisation/diversification of banks.
- Emergence of new institutions such as primary dealers and mutual funds.
- Withdrawal of reserve requirements on inter-bank borrowings.
- Withdrawal of credit controls and excessively high reserve requirements.
- Deregulation and development of markets.
- Moves toward privatisation of financial services.
- Easing of restrictions in respect of banks' foreign currency investments.
- Easing of restrictions on current and capital account convertibility.
- Lowering of entry barriers/limits on participation of foreign banks.

These reforms have paved the way for integration among various segments of the financial system. It is widely accepted that reduction/removal of financial repression has enhanced the efficiency and potential growth of the Indian economy.

Reforms in the commercial banking sector had two distinct phases. The first phase of reforms introduced subsequent to the release of the Report of the Committee on Financial System (Chairman: M. Narasimham), 1992 focussed mainly on enabling and strengthening measures. The second phase of reforms, introduced subsequent to the recommendations of the Committee on Banking Sector Reforms (Chairman: M.

Narasimham), 1998 placed greater emphasis on structural measures and improvement in standards of disclosure and levels of transparency in order to align the Indian standards with international best practices. Reforms have brought about considerable improvements as reflected in various parameters relating to capital adequacy, asset quality, profitability and operational efficiency.

2.2 Commercial Banks

2.2.1 Pre-nationalisation Period: The year 1969 was a landmark in the history of commercial banking in India. In July of that year, the government nationalised 14 major commercial banks of the country. In April 1980, government nationalised 6 more commercial banks.

In 1951, when the First Five Year Plan (1951-56) was launched, the development of rural India was accorded the highest priority. The All India Rural Credit Survey Committee recommended the creation of a State-partnered and State-sponsored bank by taking over the Imperial Bank of India and integrating with it, the former State-owned or State-associated banks. Accordingly, an Act was passed in the Parliament in May 1955 and the State Bank of India was constituted on July 1, 1955. Later, the State Bank of India (Subsidiary Banks) Act was passed in 1959 enabling the State Bank of India to take over eight former State-associated banks as its subsidiaries.

During the pre-nationalisation period, the industrial sector claimed the lion's share in bank credit. Within the industry, the large-scale sector cornered the bulk of credit and the share of small-scale industries was marginal. There were many reasons for the dominance of large industrial companies in the banking sector. Firstly, many commercial banks were under the ownership/control of big industrial houses. Secondly, through common directors (called interlocking of directorship), many commercial banks were connected with industrial and business houses, facilitating the flow of credit to large industries. Thirdly, the established industrial houses could obtain industrial licenses easily and on that basis, appropriate long-term bank credit.

A disturbing feature of the pre-nationalisation banking policy was the negligible share of agricultural sector in bank credit. This share hovered around 2 per cent of total commercial bank credit. The privately-owned commercial banks were neither interested nor geared to meet the risky and small credit requirements of the farmers. Similarly, the share of other non-industrial sectors in bank credit was also low.

Since the commercial banks were under the control of big industrialists, the lendable funds of the banks were sometimes used to finance socially undesirable activities like hoarding of essential commodities.

2.2.2 Post-nationalisation Period: As already noted, leading commercial banks of the country were nationalised in 1969 with the following objectives in view.

- To break the ownership and control of banks by a few business families.
- To prevent concentration of wealth and economic power.
- To mobilise savings of the masses from every nook and corner of the country.
- To pay greater attention to the credit needs of the priority sectors like agriculture and small industries.

The post-nationalisation period witnessed a remarkable expansion in the banking and financial system. The biggest achievement of nationalisation was the reallocation of sectoral credit in favour of agriculture, small industries and exports which formed the core of the priority sector. Within agriculture, credit for the procurement of food grains (food credit) was a major item. Other agricultural activities preferred for credit included poultry farming, dairy, and piggeries. Certain other sectors of the economy which also received attention for credit allocation were: professionals and self-employed persons, artisans and weaker sections of society. Conversely, there was a sharp fall in bank credit to large-scale industries. However, the share of small-scale industry registered an upward trend.

Nationalisation of commercial banks was a mixed blessing. After nationalisation there was a shift of emphasis from industry to agriculture. The country witnessed rapid expansion in bank branches, even in rural areas. Branch expansion programme led to mobilisation of savings from all parts of the country. Nationalised banks were able to pay attention to the credit needs of weaker sections, artisans and self-employed. However, bank nationalisation created its own problems like excessive bureaucratisation, red-tapism and disruptive tactics of trade unions of bank employees.

2.2.3 Banking Sector Reforms since 1991: Until the early 1990s, the banking sector suffered from lack of competition, low capital base, low productivity and high intermediation cost. Prior to reforms, the Indian Government determined the quantum, allocation and the price of credit, a situation referred to as *financial repression* by some experts. It was in this backdrop, that wide-ranging banking sector reforms in India were introduced as an integral part of the economic reforms initiated in the early 1990s. Reforms in the commercial banking sector had two distinct phases.

The first phase of reforms implemented subsequent to the release of the Report of the Committee on Financial System (Chairman: M. Narasimham), 1992 (or Narasimham Committee I) focussed mainly on enabling and strengthening measures. The Committee was guided by the fundamental assumption that the resources of the banks come from the general public and held by the banks in trust. These resources have to be deployed for maximum benefit of their owners, i.e. the depositors. This assumption automatically implies that even the Government has no business to endanger the solvency, health and efficiency of the nationalised banks.

According to the Committee, the poor financial shape and low efficiency of public sector banks was due to: (a) extensive degree of central direction of their operations, particularly in terms of investment, credit allocation and branch expansion and (b) excessive political interference, resulting into failure of commercial banks to operate on the basis of their commercial judgement and in the framework of internal economy. Despite opposition from trade unions and some political parties, the Government accepted all the major recommendations of the Committee some of which have already been implemented.

The second phase of reforms, implemented subsequent to the recommendations of the Committee on Banking Sector Reforms (Chairman: M. Narasimham), 1998 (or Narasimham Committee II) placed greater emphasis on structural measures and improvement in standards of disclosure and levels of transparency in order to align the Indian standards with international best practices.

The key objective of reforms in the banking sector in India has been to enhance the stability and efficiency of banks. To achieve this objective, various reform measures were initiated that could be categorised broadly into three main groups: (a) enabling measures, (b) strengthening measures and (c) institutional measures.

Enabling measures were designed to create an environment where banks could respond optimally to market signals on the basis of commercial considerations. Salient among these included reduction in statutory pre-emptions so as to release greater funds for commercial lending, interest rate deregulation to enable price discovery, granting of operational autonomy to banks and liberalization of the entry norms for financial intermediaries.

The strengthening measures aimed at reducing the vulnerability of banks in the face of fluctuations in the economic environment. These included, inter alia, capital adequacy, income recognition, asset classification and provisioning norms, exposure norms, improved levels of transparency, and disclosure standards.

Institutional framework conducive to development of banks needs to be developed. Salient among these include reforms in the legal framework pertaining to banks and creation of new institutions.

Banking sector reforms since 1991 have included, among others, the following.

- Granting operational autonomy to banks.
- Liberalisation of entry norms for banks.
- Reduction in statutory pre-emptions so as to release greater funds for commercial lending.
- Deregulation of interest rates.
- Relaxation in investment norms for banks.
- Easing of restrictions in respect of banks' foreign currency investments.
- Withdrawal of reserve requirements on inter-bank borrowings.

Thus, financial repression has eased substantially with the deregulation of interest rates and substantial removal of credit allocation.

2.3 Development Finance Institutions (DFIs)

DFIs or simply financial institutions were set up in India at various points of time starting from the late 1940s to cater to the medium to long-term financing requirements of industry as the capital market in India had not developed sufficiently. After Independence in 1947, the national government adopted the path of planned economic development and launched the First Five Year Plan in 1951. This strategy of development provided the critical inducement for establishment of DFIs at both all-India and state-levels. In order to perform their role, DFIs were extended funds of the RBI and government guaranteed bonds, which constituted major sources of their funds. Funds from these sources were not only available at concessional rates, but also on a long-term basis with their maturity period ranging from 10-15 years. On the asset side, their operations were marked by near absence of competition.

A large variety of financial institutions have come into existence over the years to perform various types of financial activities. While some of them operate at all-India level, others are state level institutions. Besides providing direct loans (including rupee loans, foreign currency loans), financial institutions also extend financial assistance by way of underwriting and direct subscription and by issuing guarantees. Recently, some DFIs have started extending short-term/working capital finance, although term-lending continues to be their primary activity.

Prior to financial sector reforms initiated in 1991, DFIs operated in an over-protected environment with most of the funding coming from assured sources at concessional terms. In the wake of financial sector reforms, the RBI started monitoring the functioning of DFIs with a view to impart market orientation to their operations. In tune with the emerging scenario, their access to low cost funds of the RBI was discontinued.

In spite of the withdrawal of concessional funds, operations of DFIs were not adversely affected during the early years of the reform, as there were several factors that worked to their advantage. Lending interest rates both for banks and DFIs were deregulated in the early 1990s. However, this was the period when the inflation rate was very high. As a result, interest rates ruled very high. While the marginal cost of funds for DFIs increased sharply, they had the advantage of recycling some of the past concessional borrowings at high rate of interest. Taking advantage of flexibility provided to them in the matter of raising and deploying external commercial borrowings, DFIs also raised significant funds from the international market. In view of the booming conditions in the domestic capital market, some of the DFIs could also raise resources successfully both by way of debt and equity at handsome premia. On the asset side, there was a good demand for funds due to acceleration of economic activity in general and industrial sector in particular.

On their part, DFIs took several steps to reposition themselves and reorient their operations in the new competitive environment. They have diversified their activities into new areas of business such as investment banking, stock broking and other fee and commission based business. Nevertheless, their business has slowed down and their operations have become less profitable. The Committee on Banking Sector Reforms (Chairman: M. Narasimham), 1998 recommended that DFIs should, over a period of time, convert themselves into banks or non-banking financial companies (NBFCs). It is noteworthy that ICICI, one of the leading DFIs, has merged with the ICICI Bank.

Financial institutions, which constitute an important source of funds for the commercial sector, have been losing ground fast. The situation has come about as a result of the distinction between development and commercial banking getting blurred, high cost of funds and asset-liability mismatches. With reforms in the financial sector, the facility of low cost funds under long-term operations funds, funds from bilateral and multilateral agencies and bond issues under statutory liquidity ratio is no more available. Now the financial institutions are raising funds at market-related rates of interest. The RBI had advised financial institutions to chart a path for their evolution into universal banks. The merger of ICICI with the ICICI Bank was approved by the RBI in April 2002. The merger was approved subject to ICICI fulfilling conditions relating to reserve requirements and prudential norms after the merger. Lately, DFIs have taken several steps to reposition themselves and reorient their operations in the competitive environment by offering innovative products and diversifying their activities into new areas of business (such as investment banking, stock broking, custodial services, etc.) so as to harness the synergies and to reduce the risk arising out of narrow specialization.

As a result of liberalization of trade and industrial sectors, competition in the commodity market increased. While some companies were able to cope with the increased competition effectively, some others were not. This also had an adverse effect on the asset quality of DFIs. In a declining interest rate scenario, high cost of funds raised by DFIs in the past became a cause of concern. As a result, some of the DFIs by exercising call option redeemed the long-term bonds long before their final maturity. Competition on the asset side also increased with some banks stepping up their project finance activity. All these factors have significantly impinged on the profitability of DFIs. As DFIs have high NPAs, they would be required to provide for them, which is likely to put a further pressure on their profitability.

The RBI in the Discussion Paper released in January 1999 indicated that DFIs should have the freedom to retain their status and specialize in their own activities. However, if a DFIs chooses to become a bank, that option should also be available. In response to interest evinced by DFIs, the RBI issued guidelines setting out various operational and regulatory parameters that need to be complied with by DFIs if they are to become banks. ICICI, one of the major DFIs, along with two of its subsidiaries has merged with the ICICI Bank. However, to fill the void being created by the disappearance of DFIs, urgent steps are required to be taken to develop the private corporate debt market and introduce appropriate instruments to reduce the risk arising out of long term financing by other players such as banks.

In short, DFIs were set up with the specific objective of meeting the medium to long-term requirement of funds. However, DFIs in the present form are finding it difficult to sustain their operations. Their business has slowed down and their operations have become less profitable. This has raised issues relating to the viability of DFIs.

Historically, the RBI and the Central Government have played a major role in financing DFIs by subscribing to the share capital, by allowing them to issue Government guaranteed bonds and by extending long-term loans at concessional terms. However, with the financial sector reforms in the 1990s, concessional lending by the RBI and the Government was phased out, leaving the financial institutions to rely for financing their needs on the equity capital and the debt markets. Expansion of their equity base through public offers and public issues of long-term bonds has become an important element of their market-based financing. In order to provide flexibility, the RBI has also allowed DFIs to raise resources by way of term deposits. In order to expand their scope of business, a large number of them have been entering into various businesses, viz. venture capital, mutual funds, banking and insurance.

The RBI started monitoring the operations of DFIs in 1990 with the objective of having an integrated view of the operations of financial institutions and commercial banks and for providing a more comprehensive basis for the conduct of monetary and credit policies. DFIs were brought within the supervisory jurisdiction of the Board for Financial Supervision from 1994.

The setting up of specialised financial institutions and refinance institutions provided depth to financial intermediation outside the banking sector. Of late a number of financial institutions have diversified into several new activities, such as investment banking, infrastructure financing, and providing guarantees for domestic and offshore lending for infrastructure projects. Coupled with increased financial market liberalization, these developments have enhanced competition in the Indian financial system.

Profitability of DFIs, in general, has declined after the initiation of reforms in 1991. The decline in profitability is attributable to increased competition on the asset side and increased cost of funds on the liability side after assured sources of funds were withdrawn. Thus, insofar as financial intermediaries are concerned, reforms have had a mixed impact. While reforms have brought about significant improvement in respect of commercial banks, the impact is not so perceptible in respect of co-operative banks and non-bank financial intermediaries.

DFIs, which have traditionally played an important role in

financing investment activity, are finding themselves at crossroads. In the initial phase of reforms, DFIs were able to sustain their business and profitability due to several factors, which worked to their advantage. However, on the whole, they have not been able to sufficiently reposition themselves in the changed operating environment. While all DFIs are able to maintain adequate CRAR, the profitability and asset quality of some of them are becoming a cause of concern.

Taking into account the difficulties faced by AIFIs in the changed operating environment, the RBI constituted a Working Group on Development Financing Institutions (Chairman: N. Sadasivan). The Working Group submitted its report in May, 2004 suggesting a roadmap for development financing and the role of DFIs. The main recommendations made by the Working Group relate to conversion of DFIs, which are inherently unsustainable, into either a bank or an NBFC, strengthening of regulatory framework, raising of risk weightage of certain categories of investment from 20 per cent to 100 per cent and extension of certain relaxations for DFIs for converting into banks for a period of 3 to 5 years after their conversion. With the progressive blurring of functions between banks and financial institutions, the AIFIs are fast losing ground and adopting the business model of a bank to remain viable in the long run. The merger of ICICI with ICICI bank on March 30, 2002 was the beginning of this trend.

2.4 Non-banking Financial Companies (NBFCs) and Mutual Funds

2.4.1 NBFCs: NBFCs are financial intermediaries which provide a variety of services including equipment leasing, hire purchase, loans, investments and chit fund activities. This sector comprises a heterogeneous lot of privately-owned, small-sized financial intermediaries. These companies play an important role in providing credit to the unorganised sector and to the small borrowers at the local level. Hire purchase finance is by far the largest activity of NBFCs.

Although NBFCs in India have existed for a long time.

they shot into prominence in the second half of the 1980s and in the first-half of the 1990s, as deposits raised by them grew rapidly. Customer orientation, concentration in the main financial centres and attractive rates of return offered by them are some of the reasons for their rapid growth. Primarily engaged in the area of retail banking, they face competition from banks and financial institutions.

With the increasing services sector activity in India, the NBFCs have been playing a critical role in providing credit. NBFCs have extensive networks.

In India, four types of non-banking financial companies (NBFCs), *viz.* equipment leasing companies, hire-purchase companies, loan companies and investment companies are under the regulatory purview of the RBI. The insertion of chapter III B in the Reserve Bank of India Act, 1934 enabled the RBI to regulate the NBFCs statutorily from February 1964. Since then, the RBI has initiated a series of measures to appropriately regulate and supervise the NBFCs according to the need from time to time.

In 1966, two new directives, *viz.* the Non-Banking Financial Companies (Reserve Bank) Directions, 1966 and Non-Banking Non-Financial Companies (Reserve Bank) Directions, 1966 were issued to increase the regulatory powers of the RBI with regard to NBFCs.

During 1973-74, the RBI issued Miscellaneous Non-Banking Companies (Reserve Bank) Directions, 1973 to regulate the acceptance of deposits by the companies conducting prize chits, lucky draws, savings scheme etc. The Reserve Bank of India (Amendment) Act, 1974 empowered the RBI to inspect NBFCs, whenever the RBI considers such inspection is necessary or expedient. In May 1987, the RBI issued Residuary Non-Banking Companies (Reserve Bank) Directions, 1987 to regulate such companies.

In pursuance of the recommendations of the Working Group on NBFCs in 1992 (Chairman: A.C. Shah), the RBI initiated a series of regulatory measures.

In 1994, NBFCs were subjected to prudential norms relating to income recognition, asset classification, provisioning and capital adequacy. Accordingly, registered NBFCs were required to achieve a minimum capital adequacy norm of 6 per cent in March 31, 1995. The CRAR norms for NBFCs have been progressively increased and the norm prescribed at present is 12 per cent.

However, keeping in view various systemic issues, the need was felt for further strengthening the regulatory and supervisory framework for NBFCs. Accordingly, the Reserve Bank of India (Amendment) Act was enacted in 1997. It conferred extensive powers on the RBI for regulation and supervision of NBFCs. Given the immense diversity among NBFCs, norms were strengthened particularly for public deposits.

Prior to the Reserve Bank (Amendment) Act, 1997, there was lack of adequate regulation and supervision mechanism for most types of NBFCs. It is true that NBFCs were regulated by the RBI but the focus of the latter was mainly on the liability side. Following this Amendment, a comprehensive regulatory framework for NBFCs sector was put in place. The regulatory framework was tightened further. Non-submission of periodic returns to RBI by NBFCs is a common feature. To address this problem, RBI decided to impose penalties besides considering cancellation of certificate of registration of NBFCs having deposits of Rs. 50 crore and above.

The Amended Act also prescribed the revised entry point norms, compulsory registration with the RBI, maintenance of certain percentage of liquid assets in the form of unencumbered approved securities, formulating a reserve policy and transferring certain proportion of profits every year.

In order to ensure that the depositors are served appropriately and systemic risks are avoided, the current focus of the RBI is on improving their functioning, including transparency of operations, corporate governance, Know Your Customer rules etc. The NBFCs registered with the RBI that have net owned funds of Rs. 5 crore and more have been permitted to undertake insurance business as agent of insurance companies on a fee basis, without any risk participation. A minimum 12 per cent capital adequacy for NBFCs, which want to enter into insurance joint ventures, has been prescribed. If the company holds public deposits, the minimum capital adequacy has been proposed at 15 per cent. Further, minimum net worth requirement of Rs. 500 crore, three years of continuous net profit, and maximum non-performing assets of 5 per cent of the total outstanding leased/hire purchase assets and advances have been prescribed for NBFCs.

In the wake of failure of some NBFCs and loss of depositors' money, the supervision of NBFCs assumed critical importance. In the backdrop of the recommendations of the Khanna Committee (1999), a comprehensive supervisory model has been devised for effective supervision of the NBFCs depending upon the size, type of activity and acceptance or otherwise of public deposits. For this purpose, a four-pronged mechanism comprising on-site inspection on the CAMELS pattern, off-site monitoring through periodic control returns using state-of-the-art information technology; an effective market intelligence network; and a system of submission of exception reports by statutory auditors of NBFCs were instituted in order to buttress the regulatory and supervisory framework for NBFCs.

The system of on-site examination is structured on the basis of CAMELS approach and the same is akin to the supervisory model adopted for the banking system. The inspection policy for the NBFCs has recently been revised to regulate them effectively. In order to bring the functioning of the NBFCs in line with international best practices, the RBI initiated a consultative process with the NBFCs with regard to their plan of action for voluntarily phasing out of their acceptance of public deposits. Recently, the RBI has laid down a road map for Residuary Non-Banking Companies (RNBCs) with a view to ensure that the transition process of these institutions complies with the RBI's directions.

The RBI issued detailed guidelines for the merger/amalgamation in respect of the private sector banks on May 11, 2005. These guidelines are applicable to merger proposals between two banking entities or between a banking company and non-banking financial company (NBFC); the same governing principles would be applicable, as appropriate, to public sector banks (PSBs) also. The merger of an NBFC with a banking entity would be subject to satisfaction of the Board of the banking entity on certain safeguards such as

- whether the NBFC has violated/is likely to violate any of the RBI/Securities and Exchange Board of India (SEBI) norms and if so, ensure that these norms are complied with before the scheme of amalgamation is approved;
- the NBFC has complied with the Know Your Customer (KYC) norms for the accounts, which will become accounts of the banking entity after amalgamation; and
- if the NBFC has availed of credit facilities from bankers/financial institutions (FIs), then the consent of the banks/FIs concerned for the proposed merger/amalgamation would be needed.

In June 2000, NBFCs registered with the RBI were permitted, with prior approval of the RBI, to set up insurance joint ventures for undertaking insurance business with risk participation and also to undertake insurance business as agents of insurance companies on a fee basis, without any risk participation subject to satisfaction of some eligibility criteria. This facility was later extended to financial institutions in November 2001.

In February 2004, it was decided to allow NBFCs registered with the RBI to take up insurance agency business on a fee basis and without risk participation, without the approval of the RBI subject to certain conditions.

There are, however, indications that the reform process has not as yet resulted in any noticeable improvement in the operational efficiency of NBFCs. In fact profitability position has showed some signs of deterioration in recent years. Similarly, operations of NBFCs have witnessed significant changes especially on the liability side. With the tightening of regulations, many of the NBFCs with insufficient capital base have been weeded out. This combined with the tightening of regulations for raising deposits has resulted in reduction in size of this sector.

As NBFCs provide important services in certain niche areas of the financial sector, improvement in the efficiency of these entities is of crucial importance. The RBI has continued to pursue with various State Governments the case for enacting legislation for protection of interest of depositors in financial establishments. Creating public awareness about activities and risk-profile of NBFCs is yet another important area, which needs to be focussed upon. Improvement in corporate governance practices and financial disclosures by NBFCs also need to be focused upon in future.

2.4.2 Mutual Funds: Mutual funds are very popular all over the world and they play an important role in the financial system of many countries. Mutual funds are an ideal medium for investment by small investors in the stock market. Mutual funds pool together the investments of small investors for participation in the stock market. Being institutional investors, mutual funds can afford market analysis generally not available to individual investors. Furthermore, mutual funds can diversify the portfolio in a better way as compared with individual investors due to the expertise and availability of funds.

Until 1987, Unit Trust of India (UTI) was the only mutual fund in the country. In that year another mutual fund, sponsored by a public sector bank, was established. As part of financial sector reforms, the mutual fund industry was opened to the private sector in 1993. Since then, the expansion of mutual fund business has intensified competition and led to product innovation. Mutual funds presently offer a variety of options to investors such as income funds, balanced funds, liquid funds, gift funds, index funds, exchange traded funds, sectoral funds etc. The deceleration in the growth of mutual funds in the 1990s could be attributed partly to the relatively poor performance of the stock markets and partly due to withdrawal of tax benefits under Section 80M of the Indian Income Tax Act, 1961.

Some of the mutual funds had offered assured return schemes enabling them to mobilize large resources. A number of mutual funds faced difficulties in meeting their redemption obligations relating to such schemes. In several cases, the sponsors of mutual funds had to infuse additional funds to meet the shortfall. As a result, mutual funds, by and large, discontinued the floatation of assured return schemes, which had some dampening effect on the resource mobilization by mutual funds.

While most of the mutual funds were somehow able to meet their commitments on account of assured return schemes, UTI faced a somewhat different problem on two different occasions between October 1998 and July 2001. US-64, which was the flagship scheme of UTI and enjoyed the investors' faith, first faced problem in December 1998 when the reserves under the scheme were reported negative. In order to restore investors' confidence, several measures were initiated by the Government/UTI. While these measures helped the US-64 to make a turnaround, the problem resurfaced again in July 2001 when UTI slashed down the dividend rates for the year 2000-01 and suspended sales and repurchases of US-64 for a period of 6 months from July 2001 to December 2001. This created a crisis of confidence and to restore investors' confidence various measures were initiated again, which culminated in splitting the UTI into two parts: UTI-I and UTI-II.

On October 28, 2002, an ordinance was promulgated which repealed the UTI Act, and created two entities, UTI-1 and UTI-2. UTI-2 is an unencumbered mutual fund, with only NAV-based schemes. UTI-1 has US-64 and the assured returns schemes. On January 15, 2003, the handover of UTI-2 to a new set of owners (State Bank of India, Bank of Baroda, Punjab National Bank and Life Insurance Corporation of India) took place.

The problem with US-64 scheme of UTI adversely affected the resource mobilization by mutual funds in general and UTI in particular. On both the occasions, when UTI faced difficulties and while resource mobilization by UTI declined sharply, private sector mutual funds were able to fill the gap created by UTI only partially as overall mobilization by all mutual funds on both the occasions declined sharply after the occurrence of the problem.

In March 2002, guidelines were issued to enable mutual funds to invest in rated securities in countries with fully convertible currencies. This marked an important milestone, through which mutual funds will be able to deliver better risk/return tradeoffs through international diversification.

Mutual funds are an ideal vehicle for investment by retail investors in the stock market for several reasons. First, it pools the investments of small investors together, increasing thereby the participation in the stock market. Secondly, mutual funds, being institutional investors, can afford market analysis by experts generally not available or accessible to individual investors, providing thereby informed decisions to the small investors. Thirdly, mutual funds can diversify the portfolio in a better way as compared with individual investors due to the expertise and availability of funds.

Mutual funds in India, because of their small size and slower growth in the recent past, have tended to play only a limited role in the stock market.

In view of small size of their operations, mutual funds in normal times hardly exert any influence on the stock market. Nonetheless, major developments concerning mutual funds do exert significant influence on the sentiment. The negative developments at UTI such as reporting of negative corpus for US-64 in October 1998, heavy redemption pressure on US-64 units in July 2001 etc. resulted in decline in the BSE Sensex. On the other hand, positive developments like implementation of special unit scheme and announcement of positive corpus for US-64 were associated with general uptrend in the equity prices.

Penetration of mutual funds in the rural areas remains small. Mutual funds have been found to be popular mainly with the middle and high-income groups and have not been found to be an attractive investment avenue for the low-income groups. Thus, if mutual funds have to grow fast, they would need to devise appropriate schemes to attract the saving of low-income groups, especially in rural areas. This is the only way to ensure participation of all categories of investors into the capital market, which is so crucial for its long-term development. Mutual funds with large funds at their disposal are also required to act as a counterweight to Foreign Institutional Investors (FIIs), which generally exert a significant influence on the stock market.

Although reforms in the financial sector since 1991 have been successful in creating a competitive environment, the growth of mutual funds has slowed down, partly due to the problems faced by UTI.

2.5 Money Market

An understanding of the organisational structure of markets for financial assets is vital for knowing the limitations and prospects with regards to efficiency, integration and stability. Financial markets are at the core of the transmission mechanism of monetary policy. In India, financial markets have been developed with a specific emphasis on increasing allocative efficiency of resources and promoting financial stability.

Financial markets in India comprise, in the main: the money market, Government securities market, capital market, insurance market, and the foreign exchange market. Recently, the derivatives market has also emerged. With banks having already been allowed to undertake insurance business, bancassurance market has also emerged in a big way.

Till the early 1990s, most of the financial markets were characterised by controls over the pricing of financial assets, restrictions on flows or transactions, barriers to entry, low liquidity and high transaction costs. These characteristics came in the way of development of the markets and allocative efficiency of resources channelled through them. From 1991 onward, financial market reforms have emphasised the strengthening of the price discovery process, easing restrictions on transactions, reducing transaction costs and enhancing systemic liquidity.

Money market is the most important segment of the financial system as it provides the fulcrum for equilibrating short-term demand for and supply of funds, thereby facilitating the conduct of monetary policy. It is a market for short-term funds with a maturity of up to one year and includes financial instruments that are close substitutes for money. The main instruments comprising the money market are: (a) call money/notice money, (b) certificates of deposit (CDs), (c) treasury bills (abolished with effect from April 1997), (d) repurchase agreements (repos), (e) commercial bills, (f) commercial paper (CPs), and (g) inter-corporate funds.

While inter-bank money markets and central bank lending via repo operations or discounting, provide liquidity for banks, private non-bank money market instruments, such as commercial bills and commercial paper provide liquidity to the commercial sector. Unlike in developed economies where money markets are promoted by financial intermediaries out of efficiency considerations, in India, as in many other developing countries, the evolution of the money market and its structure has been integrated into the overall deregulation process of the financial sector.

The money market is generally expected to perform three broad functions.

- It provides an equilibrating mechanism to even out

demand for and supply of short-term funds.

- It also presents a focal point for central bank intervention for influencing liquidity and general level of interest rates in the economy.
- It provides reasonable access to providers and users of short-term funds to fulfil their borrowing and investment requirements at an efficient market clearing price.

The RBI is the most important constituent of the money market. Owing to its implications for conducting monetary policy, the money market falls under the direct purview of regulation of the RBI. The primary objective of the RBI's operations in the money market has been to ensure that short-term interest rates and liquidity are maintained at levels which are consistent with the overall monetary policy objectives, *viz.* maintaining price stability, ensuring adequate flow of credit to the productive sectors of the economy and maintaining orderly conditions in the financial markets. Liquidity and interest rates in the system are influenced by the RBI through the use of various instruments at its disposal which, *inter alia*, include (a) cash reserve ratio, (b) standing facilities/refinance schemes, (c) repo and reverse repo transactions, (d) changes in the Bank Rate, (e) open market operations and (f) foreign exchange swap operations.

Recognising the important role of the market in the monetary policy process, the RBI has taken active interest in continuously refining the money market instruments in order to have greater control over the liquidity in the system and for creating an efficient mechanism to impart interest rate signals.

The money market in India witnessed significant progress particularly from the mid-1990s, in terms of refinements in money market instruments, introduction of new instruments and supplementary measures to add depth and liquidity to the market.

During the 1990s, the participation in the call money market was widened to cover primary and satellite dealers and corporates (through primary dealers) besides other participants. While banks and primary dealers are permitted to lend and borrow in the market, other entities can participate only as lenders. Following the recommendations of the Committee on Banking Sector Reforms (Chairman: M. Narasimham), 1998 and the RBI's Internal Working Group to Examine the Development of Call Money Market (1997), steps were initiated to reform the call money market and make it a pure inter-bank market, in a phased manner starting in 1999. With the development of the repo market since the late 1990s, the call money market has gradually been transformed into a pure inter-bank market including primary dealers. This process, which was initiated in 1999, was completed in August 2005.

A significant development in the Indian money market has been the introduction of Rupee derivatives, i.e. Interest Rate Swaps (IRS)/ Forward Rate Agreements (FRA) in 1999 to further deepen the money market and enable market participants to hedge their risks. In addition to several other measures taken since its introduction, with effect from May 20, 2005, market participants were advised to use only domestic Rupee benchmarks for interest rate derivatives. Market participants were, however, given a transition period of six months for using Mumbai Inter-bank Forward Offered Rate (MIFOR) as a benchmark, subject to review. However, on request from the Fixed Income Money Market and Derivatives Association (FIMMDA), market participants have been allowed to use MIFOR swaps in respect of transactions having underlying permissible forex exposures, for market making purpose, subject to appropriate limit as may be approved by the RBI.

Following the recommendations of the Technical Group on Money Market (May 2005), the focus and policy thrust of the RBI in the money market has been towards encouraging the growth of collateralised market, ensuring transparency and better price discovery, providing avenues for better risk management and strengthening monetary operations.

Although significant progress has been made through initiation of various reforms, there are several issues, which need to be addressed. While the overnight market is reasonably developed, the term-money market is yet to develop necessitating large rollover of short-term funds in the overnight market. This is mainly on account of the inability of participants to form appropriate interest rate expectations in the medium-term due to which there is a tendency on their part to look themselves into a short-term period. Furthermore, overwhelming preference of corporates for *cash* credit rather than for *loan* credit generally forces banks to deploy a large amount in the call/notice money market rather than in the term money market.

Another issue relates to the avenues available to deploy short-term funds to non-bank corporates. A critical issue in transforming the call/notice money market into a pure inter-bank market is the availability of some other avenue for short-term funds for non-bank participants. The commercial bill market continues to be limited, especially as few participants are willing to bear the concomitant risk of default. Thus, the repo trade at this stage offers a quick medium for developing a market for short-term funds especially as the transactions are collateralised in the case of non-banks. While the RBI has taken several steps to develop a repo market for non-bank participants, a vibrant repo market is, however, yet to develop. There is also a need to develop uniform accounting and documentation procedures in this regard.

Money market in India, which traditionally consisted largely of call/notice money market, now comprises, many other instruments such as CPs, CDs, repos and FRAs/IRS. Various reform measures have helped in improving the depth and efficiency of money market operations. The operationalisation of the LAF has provided an informal corridor for overnight call money borrowing rate, which has further imparted stability and flexibility in the interest rate structure and to the market. The other money market instruments such as CPs and CDs have also been developed through alignment in maturity (with deposit instruments like term deposits) and easing of issuance norms. With proper development of other money market segments, non-banks have been able to smoothly switch over from the call/notice money market to other segments.

The RBI's approach has been to foster balanced development of different segments of the money market, introduce new instruments and make the existing instruments more flexible, reduce dependence of participants on uncollateralised exposures, facilitate price discovery in the short-end and upgrade the payment system infrastructure. Accordingly, the RBI's strategy has focused on developing pure call/notice money market, instituting full-fledged Liquidity Adjustment Facility, developing infrastructure, promoting transparency, and initiating various measures pertaining to instruments for non-bank participants. Following the various initiatives taken by the RBI over the years, the depth and liquidity in the money market has increased significantly.

2.6 Capital Market

Capital market is a market for long-term funds. The distinction between capital market and money market is not watertight. Broadly speaking, capital market focuses on financing of fixed investment (machinery and equipment) while money market provides working capital finance (raw material etc.)

Capital market channelises household savings to the corporate sector and allocates funds to firms. In this process, it allows both firms and households to share risks associated with business. Moreover, capital market enables the valuation of firms on an almost continuous basis and plays an important role in the governance of the corporate sector.

An efficient capital market is an important constituent of a sound financial system. In India, efforts have been made in recent years to set up an effective regulatory framework covering major participants in the capital market. Similarly, the technology of trading and settlements in the stock exchanges has been upgraded. Internet-based trading in securities has been permitted. Foreign institutional investors (FIIs) and pension funds were allowed to enter the Indian stock market from 1993 onwards.

A stock (or share) market deals mainly in corporate securities. The securities are chiefly in the form of equity shares and debentures. The purpose of these securities is to raise long-term funds for companies engaged in production. The function of the stock market is two-fold: (a) to arrange for the raising of new capital (primary market function) and (b) to provide liquidity to existing securities (secondary market function).

The new capital is raised by the issue of shares and debentures. The corporate enterprises raising new capital may be new companies or existing companies planning expansion of their operations. Sometimes, existing private firms go public, i.e. become public limited companies.

The stock market helps the floatation of new issues by providing a variety of services like underwriting, distribution, and listing of the issue. Underwriting means guaranteeing the purchase of a fixed amount of new issues by the underwriter. The new issues of capital may be a public issue or a rights issue or both in certain proportions. It may be in the form of equity shares or debentures. Debentures, in turn, may be fully convertible, partly convertible, or non-convertible into shares. A public issue implies that the general public is invited to subscribe to the new issue. A rights issue is restricted for subscription by existing shareholders.

Stock market provides facilities for secondary market, i.e. transaction in existing securities. People desirous of converting their cash into securities can go to the stock exchange and buy securities with the help of brokers there. Similarly, securities can be converted into cash by selling them in the market.

Transactions in the secondary market reflect the investment climate in the economy.

Prior to the onset of financial sector reforms in 1991, the capital market structure in India was subject to several controls and opaque procedures. The trading and settlement system was outdated and not in tune with international practices. Raising of capital from the market was regulated by the Capital Issues (Control) Act, 1947 which was administered by the Controller of Capital Issues (CCIs) in the Ministry of Finance, Government of India. The scheme of controls under the Act required all the companies to obtain prior consent for issues of capital to the public. Pricing as well as the features of the capital structure (such as debt-equity ratios), were controlled by the Government. Similarly, the Securities Contracts (Regulation) Act was administered by the Directorate of Stock Exchanges also in the Ministry of Finance. It empowered the Government to recognise/derecognise stock exchanges, stipulate rules and bye-laws for their functioning, compel listing of securities by public companies etc. Such a system of regulation and control was fragmented and inadequate in the context of liberalisation wave sweeping across the world. Urgent measures were needed to relax controls and modernise the functioning of capital market

In 1992, the Capital Issues (Control) Act, 1947 was repealed and the office of the Controller of Capital Issues (CCIs) was abolished. SEBI was set up in April 1988 by an administrative order and acquired a statutory status in 1992. With this ended all controls related to raising of funds from the market. Issuers of capital, however, are required to meet the guidelines of SEBI on disclosures and protection of investors. The move was aimed at enhancing the efficiency, safety, integrity and transparency of the market.

SEBI has emerged as an autonomous and independent statutory body with a definite mandate which requires it to (a) protect the interest of the investors in securities, (b) promote the development of the securities market and (c) regulate the securities market.

The SEBI prohibits fraudulent and unfair trade practices, including insider trading. It also regulates substantial acquisition of shares and takeovers. In order to ensure protection of investors and to safeguard the integrity of the markets, there is a comprehensive surveillance system. Stock exchanges are the primary targets for detection of market manipulation, price rigging and other regulatory breaches regarding capital market functioning.

In order to achieve these objectives, SEBI exercises powers under

- the SEBI Act,
- the Securities Contracts (Regulation) Act,
- the Depositories Act and
- the delegated powers under the Companies Act.

The SEBI regulates and supervises the securities market through its various regulations, guidelines and schemes issued from time to time.

In the equity market, major structural reforms included the completion of the move to rolling settlement, and the start of the equity derivatives market. On the bond market, the recent reforms have consisted of controlling settlement risks in the telephone market, using the new Clearing Corporation of India Ltd (CCIL), and initiating a new transparent, screen-based market for secondary market trading in Government of India bonds. These changes have taken place in the backdrop of significant market volatility owing to developments in the economy.

Raising of capital from the securities market before 1992 was regulated under the Capital Issues (Control) Act, 1947. Firms were required to obtain approval from the Controller of Capital Issues (CCI) for raising resources in the market. New companies were allowed to issue shares only at par. Only the existing companies with substantial reserves could issue shares at a premium, which was based on some prescribed formula. In 1992, the Capital Issues (Control) Act, 1947 was repealed and with this ended all controls related to raising of resources from the market. Since then the issuers of securities can raise capital from the market without requiring any consent from any authority, either for making the issue or for pricing it. Restrictions on rights and bonus issues have also been removed. New as well as established companies are now able to price their issues according to their assessment of market conditions. However, issuers of capital are required to meet the guidelines of SEBI on disclosure and investor protection. Companies issuing capital are required to make sufficient disclosures, including justification of the issue price and also material disclosure about the risk factors in their offer prospectus. These guidelines have served as an important measure for protecting the interest of investors and promoting the development of the primary market along sound lines.

The central goal of securities markets is to obtain a widely-dispersed ownership and trading in securities. There is conflict of interest between the management team, which controls the firm, and the shareholders, who run the firm. Many policy efforts in recent years have been devoted towards improving incentives to managers to maximize the interests of shareholders.

Improvements in disclosure are a central tool for containing the conflicts of interest between the managers and shareholders. In order to foster improvements in disclosure, SEBI set up a system named Electronic Data Information Filing and Retrieval (EDIFAR) in July 2002. This system offers a mechanism through which firms would electronically file mandatory disclosures to SEBI, and these documents would be available to individuals over the internet, with a near-zero delay. It is envisaged that in the future, disclosure would take place through company websites, exchange websites, and EDIFAR.

In order to bring greater transparency to the debt market, and to move away from bilateral negotiation towards anonymous order-matching, trading in government bonds began on stock exchanges on January 16, 2003. This has involved exploiting the identical process flow used for trading in equities. Trade takes place by anonymous order matching for all orders across the country, risk management is done by the clearing corporation, and settlement takes place at the depository. Under this system, government bonds appear in the depository statement of an investor alongside corporate equities and bonds. This system has several strengths.

- Anonymous trading avoids the supervisory and regulatory difficulties of the telephone market, where counterparties are aware of identities and can engage in trades at off-market prices.
- This market design offers symmetric market access from locations all over India and over the internet, as opposed to the telephone market, which favours entities in south Bombay.
- It exploits information technology to guarantees that orders are matched against the best price available in the country. This is in contrast with the telephone market, where traders can search for counterparties, but are not sure of having found the best counter party.
- It is fully transparent in that orders and trades are visible in real time. This is in contrast with the telephone market, where orders are not visible, and the transparency of trades is limited and delayed.
- It exploits the information technology of the depositories of the equity market (NSDL and CDSL), which have the full range of functionality required for investors such as a wide network of IT-enabled depository participants. Internet access, strong computer security, access to data about the beneficial owner down to the end-investor etc.

There is a substantial scale of securities issuance taking place through the private placement route. The private placement route has become a mechanism where securities can be placed with a few wholesale buyers of securities, without incurring the overheads of the public issue. SEBI is working on devising clear institutional mechanisms through which some public disclosure is made about these issues, while preserving the rights of issuers to not use the public issue route if it is considered to involve excessive overhead costs.

The National Stock Exchange (NSE) introduced screen-based trading at its inception in 1992 which was followed by other stock exchanges. Screen-based trading makes on-line, electronic, anonymous and order-driven transactions possible. It is a transparent system which provides equal access to all investors, irrespective of their geographical locations.

The move to an electronic trading system has resulted in transparency in trades, better price discovery and lower transaction costs. The efficiency of the market has improved through faster execution of trades. The operational efficiency of the stock market has also been strengthened through improvements in the clearing and settlement practices and the risk management process. Almost the entire delivery of securities now takes place in dematerialised form. Over the past few years or so, there has been no instance of postponement or clubbing of settlements at two main stock exchanges (BSE and NSE) despite defaults by brokers. The cases of bad deliveries are close to nil. The setting up of trade/settlement guarantee funds in most of the exchanges has considerably reduced settlement risks for investors. Corporate governance practices and disclosure norms have led to transparency in information flows, which in turn have improved the price discovery process.

Following the enactment of the Depository Act, 1996, two depositories were set up: Central Depository Services Ltd. (CDSL) and National Securities Depository Limited (NSDL). The CDSL and NSDL have been successful in the dematerialization of securities almost to the full extent. Presently, the transfer of ownership is mostly done through book-entry form. This has greatly improved the speed, accuracy and security of the settlement system. Prior to these arrangements, the settlement cycle was as high as 14 days for specified scrips and 30 days for others. The settlement risk was very high because of unforeseen happenings between the transaction and the settlement. To begin with, the settlement cycle was reduced to a week. Thereafter, rolling settlement was introduced on a T+5 basis in July 2001. From December 2001, all scrips which had established connectivity with the above-mentioned Depositories were moved to rolling settlement. The settlement cycle was further reduced to T+3 in April 2002 and to T+2 in April 2003.

The recent experience of SEBI during episodes of market misconduct revealed many limitations in the legal provisions of the SEBI Act. In addition, the growing importance of the securities markets in the economy has placed new demands upon SEBI. On October 28, 2002, an ordinance was promulgated which sought to strengthen SEBI. This ordinance involved organizational strengthening of SEBI, giving SEBI more powers for investigations and penalties, and making clearer concepts like insider trading and market manipulations.

The events of market misconduct in 2001 also highlighted the need for better mechanisms through which investigations and enforcement actions could take place on the stock market. With a view to investigate such frauds, using a multidisciplinary team of experts, it was decided to set up a Serious Fraud Office (SFO) in the Department of Company Affairs.

Apart from traditional financial markets, two more markets are emerging, namely the derivatives market, and the bancassurance market.

Financial derivatives are of recent origin in India, barring trade related forward contracts in the forex market. Over the counter (OTC) as well as exchange traded derivatives have been introduced, marking an important development in the structure of financial markets in India. Forward contracts in the forex market have also been liberalized. Exchange traded derivatives tend to be more standardized and offer greater liquidity than OTC contracts, which are negotiated between counterparties and tailored to meet the needs of the parties to the contract. Exchange traded derivatives also offer centralized limits on individual positions and have formal rules for risk and burden sharing.

In India, OTC derivatives, viz. Interest Rate Swaps (IRS) and Forward Rate Agreements (FRAs) were introduced in July 1999, while one exchange traded derivatives, viz. Stock Index Futures were introduced by the two largest stock exchanges in June 2000.

The FRA is an off-balance sheet contract between two parties under which one party agrees on the start date for trade and the party that agrees, would lodge a notional deposit with the other for a specified sum of money for a specified period of time (the FRA period) at a specified rate of interest (the contract rate). The party that has agreed to make the notional deposit has, thus, sold the FRA to the other party who has bought it.

The IRS is a contract between two counter-parties for exchange interest payment for a specified period based on a notional principal amount. The notional principal is used to calculate interest payments, but is not exchanged. Only interest payments are exchanged.

The IRS and FRA were introduced with a view to deepening the money market as also to enable banks, primary dealers and financial institutions to hedge interest rate risks.

Reforms in the capital market have had a multi-dimensional impact. The significance of the capital market has improved in providing a mechanism for allocation of resources as is reflected in increase in its share in the sources of finance for the corporates. Various indicators such as reduced volatility are pointers in the direction of increase in the safety of the market. The safety of the market has also been considerably enhanced by adoption of risk management practices and the setting up of settlement guarantee funds and investor protection funds. The integrity and transparency of the market has also gone up with the wider availability of information regarding the corporates' performance. The trading and settlement framework in the Indian stock exchanges now compares favourably with the best international practices. Liquidity in the market has improved considerably.

Capital market structure has evolved over time with the market practices and conditions generally reflecting the policies put in place. Till the onset of reforms in the early 1990s, raising of resources in the primary segment of the market was subject to several controls, disallowing pricing to be determined by market conditions. Trading in the secondary market was subject to opaque practices. The trading and settlement system was outdated and out of tune with internationally followed practices. The volumes, however, increased and securities continued to exist in physical form. Physical securities also created uncertainties for investors and increased the transaction costs. Besides, long and uncertain settlement cycles created serious problems for clearing houses. Informational flows to the market participants were also deficient. As the process of price formation has to be efficient for the growth and stability of the market, it was considered necessary to orient the Securities and Exchange Board of India (SEBI) to undertake the tasks of regulation and supervision. The SEBI was, for this purpose, given statutory powers through a separate legislation in 1992.

The equity spot market has made enormous progress, with a state-of-the-art trading system, sound clearing mechanisms, and T+3 settlement at the depository. SEBI has been working towards shortening the three-day delay between the transaction date and settlement date.

The effort is constrained by the ability of the payments system to move funds across the country, and thus awaits improvements in payments infrastructure. It also requires electronic data exchange within the securities industry, which is called Straight through Processing (STP). In November 2002, a first phase of the STP implementation came about, focusing on the transaction flow between institutional investors, custodian banks and brokers. As with advanced countries, STP would allow the securities industry in India to move towards T+1 settlement, where trades of a given date would settle on the next day.

A major issue which will influence India's securities markets in the future is the challenge of globalization. RBI has increasingly moved in the direction of giving access to international diversification to institutional investors and individual investors in India. Financial intermediaries and exchanges in India will also experience global competition. There is a need for greater thought and policy initiative, in fully integrating a global perspective into the plans of firms, exchanges, regulators and policy markets.

2.7 Foreign Exchange Market

In India, the foreign exchange market is a three-level structure consisting of (a) Reserve Bank of India (RBI) at the top, (b) authorized dealers licensed by the RBI, and (c) customers (exporters, importers, companies, and other foreign exchange earners). In addition to these main market players, there are foreign exchange money changers who bring buyers and sellers together, but are not permitted to deal in foreign exchange on their own account.

Dealings in the foreign exchange market include transactions between authorized dealers and the exporters/importers and other customers, transactions among authorized dealers themselves, transactions with overseas banks and transactions between authorized dealers and the RBI.

The authorised dealers are governed by the guidelines framed by the Foreign Exchange Dealers Association of India (FEDAI).

In line with the liberalisation measures undertaken in other areas, various reform measures have been introduced in the foreign exchange market to make it liquid, vibrant, open and market determined.

The mode of exchange rate determination is of paramount importance to the development of foreign exchange market. There is no single exchange rate regime which can be considered appropriate for all countries, at all times. Though the choice of an exchange rate regime is country-specific and contingent on macroeconomic policies, there is a growing consensus globally in favour of a flexible/floating rate regime.

2.7.1 Foreign Exchange Management Act (FEMA), 1999: Realising that FERA, 1973 was not in tune with the economic reforms initiated since 1991, the Government replaced it with a new legislation, viz. Foreign Exchange Management Act (FEMA), 1999 which came into effect from June 1, 2000. FERA, 1973 remained a nightmare for 27 years for the Indian corporate world. The objective of the new legislation as stated in the preamble to the Act is *to facilitate external trade and payments and promote the orderly development and maintenance of the foreign exchange market in India*—a shift in the approach from *conservation of foreign exchange resources of the country and the proper utilization thereof* under the FERA, 1973.

Under FEMA, foreign exchange law violators are treated as civil offenders rather than as criminals as was the case under FERA, 1973. Contravention of the provisions of FEMA invites monetary penalties. Moreover, FEMA provides for a number of appellate authorities who can be approached by the aggrieved party against whom penalties have been levied. A qualitative change has been brought about in the legal framework by FEMA. The objectives of regulation have been redefined as facilitating trade and payments as well as orderly development and maintenance of foreign exchange market in India. The legal framework envisages both the developmental dimension and orderliness or stability. The legislation provides power to the government to re-impose controls if public interest warrants it.

The shift in the policy approach entailed significant

implications for the operations of the RBI. Under the new system, all current account payments except those notified by the government are eligible for appropriate foreign currency in respect of genuine transactions from the authorized dealers without any restrictions. The surrender requirements in respect of exports of goods and services continue to operate. The RBI would, however, have the necessary regulatory jurisdiction over capital account transactions.

The reforms in industrial and trade policies initiated in the early 1990s, consistent with the changing international economic and trade relations, gave rise to the need for a more conducive climate for increased inflow of foreign investment and capital to accelerate the pace of industrial growth and export promotion. The FEMA diluted the rigorous enforcement provisions of FERA, 1973. Under FEMA

- the prosecution has to prove the guilt of the accused person,
- only monetary penalty is provided for contraventions,
- contravention of FEMA provisions are dealt with under civil procedures, for which separate administrative mechanisms in the form of Compounding Rules, Adjudicating Authority, Special Director (Appeals) and Appellate Tribunal have been established and
- for each process of law a timeframe has been provided in the Act.

The concept of compounding is an important feature of FEMA. (Under the FERA, 1973 all violations were subject to separate investigation and adjudication of the Directorate of Enforcement). The FEMA provides an opportunity of seeking compounding of contraventions, in terms of which a contravener has a *suo moto* opportunity of making an application to the compounding authority seeking the contravention to be compounded. The compounding authority is required to dispose of the application within 180 days.

The Government of India, in one of the recent Notifications, has designated the RBI as the compounding authority for all contraventions under the FEMA, except for those involving *hawala* transactions for which the Directorate of Enforcement would be the compounding authority. The new procedure would provide quick and hassle-free disposal of the cases involving contravention(s) of FEMA.

2.7.2 Current Account Convertibility: Current account convertibility allows residents to make and receive trade-related payments, i.e. receive foreign currency for export of goods and services and pay foreign currency for import of goods and services like travels, medical treatment and studies abroad. In other words, it permits free inflows and outflows for all purposes other than for capital purposes.

Current account convertibility was introduced in India in August 1994 with the acceptance of the obligations under Article VIII of the IMF's Articles of Agreement. This drastic measure contributed significantly to boost India's exports. Presently, there is almost full convertibility on the current account and partial convertibility on the capital account.

2.7.3 Capital Account Convertibility (CAC): It allows freedom to make investment in foreign equity, extend loans to foreigners, buy real estate in foreign lands and vice versa. Broadly speaking, CAC allows anyone to move freely from local currency into foreign currency and back.

In India, most categories of capital account transactions like foreign direct investment, portfolio equity investment, external commercial borrowing, non-resident deposits, short-term credit and outward investment were subject to a number of restrictions prior to 1991. During this period, FDI was seen primarily as a vehicle for transfer of technology that would be costly or difficult to develop domestically. A selective policy of case-by-case approvals was designed to channel FDI into areas that required sophisticated technology; where critical production gaps existed; or where there were prospects for substantial export potential. Foreign investment in the form of foreign collaborations was also regulated. Portfolio equity investment was generally not permitted. External commercial borrowings (ECBs) required prior approval by the Government of India on a case by case basis and the permission was granted after taking into account the purpose of the borrowing, export potential of the projects, and the capacity to generate foreign exchange to meet debt service and other payments.

During the post-1991 period, the initial liberalisation of capital account transactions was an integral part of the programme to address the balance of payment crisis of 1991. Liberalisation was accompanied by exchange market reforms in order to move over to the era of market-determined exchange rate. The major reforms in the capital account were the liberalisation of FDI and portfolio equity investment. Liberalisation of FDI gathered momentum and took a definite shape with the Industrial Policy Statement, 1991 effecting significant policy liberalisation in the context of FDI. During the course of the 1990s, most sectors had been brought under the ambit of automatic approval route for FDI with permissible foreign equity participation being significantly enhanced. In 1992, foreign institutional investors (FIIs) were permitted to invest in the primary and secondary markets for listed equity securities and Indian companies were also permitted to raise funds abroad through the issue of global depository receipts (GDRs) and foreign currency convertible bonds (FCCBs).

The approach to capital account convertibility in India has been one of gradualism, treating liberalisation of the capital account as a continuous process rather than a single event. This stance has been vindicated in the wake of the Asian crisis. India has adopted a cautious approach while initiating the process of gradual capital account liberalisation in the early 1990s. Initial reform measures on the heels of the balance of payments crisis in 1991 were predominantly directed at current account convertibility leading to acceptance of obligations under Article VIII of the International Monetary Fund's (IMF) Articles of Agreement by August 1994. Subsequently, policies in regard to foreign direct investment (FDI), portfolio investment and long-term commercial borrowings were progressively liberalised. With growing consolidation of the external sector, restrictions on outflows have also been liberalised over time. There are, however, two areas, where extreme caution has been exercised:

- unlimited access to short-term external commercial borrowing for meeting working capital and other domestic requirements; and
- unrestricted freedom to domestic residents to convert their domestic bank deposits and idle assets (such as, real estate) in response to market developments or exchange rate expectations.

The policy challenges for India arising from the opening of the capital account broadly fall under two categories: (a) management of the surges in capital flows; and (b) entrenchment of preconditions that could create room for further liberalisation of the capital account.

There is a strong opinion in India in favour of cautious liberalisation, with a greater weight attached to stability. The policy in India is to approach liberalisation on capital account cautiously, gradually, in a sequenced manner, and in response to domestic monetary and financial sector developments as also the evolving international financial architecture. Like in several other emerging market economies (EMEs), liberalisation of the current account in India preceded the liberalisation of the capital account. Capital account transactions were gradually liberalised during the 1990s. Restrictions on inflows were relaxed first, with an emphasis on encouraging FDI and portfolio equity investment and discouraging short-term debt-creating inflows. In the recent period, restrictions on capital outflows have been relaxed. Convertibility of non-resident investment has all along been a basic tenet of Indian foreign investment policy, *albeit* subject to administrative procedures.

India's exchange rate policy has evolved in tandem with international and domestic developments. The period after Independence in 1947 was followed by a fixed exchange rate regime where the Indian rupee was pegged to the pound sterling on account of historic links with Britain and this was in line with the Bretton Woods System prevailing at that time. A major event was the devaluation of the Indian rupee by 36.5 per cent on June 6, 1966.

With the breakdown of Bretton Woods system in the early 1970s and the consequent switch towards a system of managed exchange rates, and with the declining share of the UK in India's trade, the Indian rupee, effective September 1975, was delinked from the pound sterling in order to overcome the weaknesses of pegging to a single currency. Even after the rupee was delinked from the pound sterling the role of the exchange rate remained muted for quite sometime given the widespread rationing of foreign exchange through an elaborate system of licensing, other quantitative restrictions and exchange control.

During the period of 1975 to 1992, the exchange rate of rupee was officially determined by the RBI within a nominal band of +/- 5 per cent of the weighted basket of currencies of India's major trading partners. The RBI performed a market-clearing role on a day-to-day basis which introduced high variability in the size of reserves. The periodic adjustments in the exchange rate were, however, not enough to maintain external competitiveness as competitor countries had undertaken significant adjustments in their exchange rates despite their lower inflation than in India. The exchange rate regime of this period can be best characterised as an adjustable nominal peg with a band, with the nominal exchange rate being the operating variable to achieve the intermediate target of a medium-term equilibrium path of the real effective exchange rate (REER).

India now has a floating rate with no fixed rate target. Daily movements are very closely watched by the RBI. The Indian forex market is relatively thin, and the declared policy of the RBI is to meet temporary demand-supply imbalances, which arise from time to time. The objective is to keep market movements orderly and ensure that there is no liquidity problem or rumour or panic-induced volatility. While the central bank of the country intervenes in the foreign exchange market, it does so primarily to prevent volatility and instability.

True, the reforms in the forex market have yielded good results, but there are some issues which need to be addressed to enhance its stability and ensure further growth

Although the turnover in the market increased considerably over the years, it still remains small. The Triennial Central Bank Survey of the Bank for International Settlements on Foreign Exchange and Derivatives Market Activity in 2001 revealed that the share of India in total global daily turnover of the foreign exchange market remained insignificant at 0.2 percent during 2001. Since the market lacks depth, the RBI has to actively intervene in the market to absorb and provide liquidity. There is, therefore, need to take steps to further develop the market so that the need for intervention by the RBI is minimised.

The market is presently skewed with a few public sector banks accounting for the major share of the merchant transactions. For development of the market on healthy lines, it is necessary to have large number of players participating in the market.

Derivatives are an important instrument of risk hedging. Although a few derivative products have been introduced, there has not been much activity in some of them, such as FRAs. There is a need to further develop a range of derivative products like forex options.

To sum up, various reforms measures initiated have resulted in significant growth of the foreign exchange market. Also, despite liberalisation of capital account and introduction of market determined exchange rate, the foreign exchange market in India remained stable during the 1990s barring a few episodes of volatility. India's exchange rate policy of managing volatility without fixed target, while allowing the underlying demand and supply conditions to determine the exchange rate, has yielded satisfactory results. Various reforms measures in the foreign exchange market have also led to the widening and deepening of the forex market in India. This is reflected in the substantial increase in the foreign exchange market turnover particularly in the inter-bank segment.

2.8 Asset Management

The asset management sector in India has been substantially liberalized and privatized, with full foreign ownership permitted in asset management companies. This has led to robust growth in the sector, with Indian asset management companies competing effectively with foreign players.

While mutual funds in India have grown rapidly, they continue to face two key challenges, namely short-term investment horizon and secondly, relatively low retail participation with a large part of mutual fund corpuses comprising deployment of corporate surpluses. There is a need for a focused ongoing investor education campaign encouraging retail investors to participate in the capital markets through the mutual fund route, as also about the merits of allocation of a portion of their savings to long-term equity investments.

Venture Capital and Private Equity (VCPE) investor pool in India comprises primarily foreign investors, and Indian investors are largely excluded from the benefits of this asset class. The reasons for this are two-fold. Firstly, unlike internationally where institutional investors constitute the primary investors in VCPE funds in addition to high net worth individuals, in India the ability of institutional investors like banks, insurance companies and pension funds to invest in this segment is constrained or non-existent. This is anomalous given that banks and insurance companies have the necessary financial expertise to undertake a risk-reward assessment of such investment proposals. Secondly, while foreign investors investing into India need not pay tax on gains from their investments due to the benefit of double taxation treaties, Indian investors in VCPE funds are taxed; through recent amendments to the tax laws, trusts used to pool VCPE monies for investment have been denied tax pass through status unless the investments are made in a few specified sectors. These factors place VCPE funds at a disadvantage to mutual funds, both in terms of access to investors as well as tax treatment. These provisions may be reviewed given the critical role played by VCPE funds in providing longer-term capital for growth and restructuring of enterprises.

2.9 Pensions Reforms

Reforms in the structure and management of pension funds are a key area of the unfinished reform agenda. Thus far, public sector entities have been invited to manage the pension funds of all new central government employees who have joined employment from January 1, 2004. In this context, it may be mentioned that private sector banks, insurance companies and mutual funds have played an important and positive role in the development and growth of the financial sector. Life insurance companies in India are already playing an important role in the pension sector through group and personal pension products. An appropriate level playing field is therefore recommended. Further, the new pension scheme should be extended expeditiously to unorganized sector employees. Similar reforms should be initiated for the existing government-managed provident funds. Finally, all categories of pension and provident funds should be permitted to diversify their investment portfolios, shifting from the current excessive share of government securities to various categories of corporate debt, securitized paper, and an appropriate proportion of equity investments. Alternate asset classes may also be considered in due course.

2.10 Conclusion

In the context of the balance of payments crisis of 1991, a

comprehensive structural and financial sector reform process was initiated in India as recommended by the Committee on the Financial System (Chairman: M. Narasimham, 1991) which became the starting point for gradual deregulation of the financial sector and development and integration of various segments of the financial market. Measures were initiated to streamline functioning of the financial system to create a sound, competitive and efficient banking system capable of meeting the increasing challenges of liberalization and globalization.

A safe and sound financial sector is a prerequisite for sustained growth of any economy. Globalization, deregulation and advances in information technology in recent years have brought about significant changes in the operating environment for banks and other financial institutions. These institutions are faced with increased competitive pressures and changing customer demands. These, in turn, have engendered a rapid increase in product innovations and changes in business strategies. While these developments have enabled improvement in the efficiency of financial institutions, they have also posed some serious risks. The regulatory and supervisory policies are, accordingly, being reshaped and reoriented to meet the challenge of containing systemic risks. In this changing milieu, the main challenge for the supervisors has been to maintain the stability of the financial system and, at the same time, provide sufficient flexibility to financial institutions so that they can respond effectively to the growing competition while taking advantage of business opportunities and technological developments.

With the liberalization of financial markets, policy authorities in India have also had to contend with episodes of financial volatility as were witnessed in some East Asian countries. Recognizing the strong complementarity between financial stability and macroeconomic stability, the operational settings for policies are being geared to dampen excessive volatility and the possible impairment of the ability of financial institutions to handle fluctuations in financial asset prices. Current macroeconomic and financial developments in the Indian economy highlight the evolving role of the financial sector in the functioning of the economy and the growing integration across financial markets.

The financial sector in the Indian economy is undergoing a transformation towards a vibrant, competitive and diversified system, with a multiplicity of financial institutions having different risk profiles intermediating in various segments of the market spectrum. The development of banking is a critical element in the agenda of financial sector reforms in India.

Note

1. Financial repression includes (a) high required reserve ratios, (b) subsidized or directed credit programmes, (c) credit rationing, (d) ceilings on deposit and (e) fixing maximum interest rates on loans.

3

IT and IT-enabled Services

3.1 Introduction

India has emerged over the last decade as the most preferred destination for outsourcing of IT services. The vibrant IT industry is contributing immensely by providing information about latest technology and international business practices. Various sectors of the Indian economy such as industry, finance, insurance, communications and transport have adopted information technology in a big way. However, agricultural sector of the economy is lagging behind in utilizing IT services. Some efforts have been made in this regard but they are by no means adequate.

Trade in Information Technology and Information Technology enabled services (IT and BPO services) has been the main driver of growth in India's trade in services in recent years. India's exports of IT and BPO services fall in three broad categories, IT services, BPO and Software products and Engineering Services.

BPO accounts for about 27 per cent of total exports. Starting out with basic data entry tasks, the industry rapidly acquired a reputation as the primary low-cost destination for voice-based customer contact/support services, finance and accounting, and a range of back-office processing activities. The past few years have seen the scope of these services expanding to include increasingly more complex processes involving rule-based decision making and research/analytics services requiring informed individual judgment and domain/vertical knowledge. Key categories within horizontal BPO services include Customer Interaction and Support (CIS), Finance and Accounting (F&A) and other related processing services, Knowledge Services, Human Resource Management

(HRM) and Procurement BPO. With experience and maturity, several providers are also beginning to develop increasing vertical specialization, thereby complementing their horizontal BPO service offerings with vertical specific services.

Currently the industry estimates that India has a pool of 1.773 million graduates suitable for IT-BPO, which is more than the combined talent pool in China and Russia. However, even to enable India to maintain its current share of worldwide IT-BPO a gap is likely to appear within a year or so between the demand and supply of suitable graduates. One reason for this is the low proportion of fresh graduates who are employable in the sector.

Much of the BPO work is of a routine nature such as customer contact services, but increasingly the outsourced jobs are getting sophisticated and industry estimate is that in 2007 the share of Knowledge Services was 15%. The main Knowledge Services already outsourced to Indian companies are animation and simulation services, data research and analytics, and litigation services. Other possibilities are in intellectual property research, medical content and services, pharmaceutical services, writing/content development services, database development services and end-to-end logistic invoice services. The big impediment in India making progress from data processing and customer contact services to knowledge process services is deficiency in qualified talent in both quantitative and qualitative terms in economics and statistics, law, medical science, pharmacy, media and English language in particular. Table 3.1 shows the growth of IT-ITES professionals in India.

3.2 Strategies of Indian IT- BPO Companies

Indian companies adopt all the modes for supply of IT services abroad. The larger companies have set up wholly owned subsidiaries in the USA, the UK and the European continent or have opened branches to facilitate the supply of services. Some of them have adopted the strategy of acquiring local companies or entering into strategic partnerships with them. They use the quality processes, innovative technologies and delivery models of acquired companies to penetrate the local market. They have permanent employees or hire consultants based in the host country.

Table 3.1: Growth of IT-ITES Professionals in India – Indian IT Sector: Knowledge Professionals Employed*

(Nos)

	2000-01	2001-02	2002-03	2003-04	2004-05	2005-06
IT, Engineering and R&D, Software Products Exports	162000	170000	205000	296000	390000	513000
ITES Sector	70000	106000	180000	216000	316000	409000
Domestic Sector	198114	246250	285000	318000	352000	365000
Total	430114	522250	670000	830000	1058000	1287000

*Does not include employee numbers in the hardware sector.

Source: Government of India, Planning Commission, *Eleventh Five Year Plan* (2007-12), Volume III, p. 253.

All four modes of supply, cross-border (Mode 1), consumption abroad (Mode 2), establishment (Mode 3) and movement of natural persons (Mode 4) are used. In the case of BPO services Mode 1 and 3 are predominant, while in the case of IT services the supplies are made substantially by means of Modes 1, 3 and 4. In the case of IT services Indian companies deploy human resources principally from India and sometimes from other foreign bases in order to provide on-site services and have also to send persons for business visits, prospecting, and sales. Whenever the supply is made through Modes 3 and 4 the investment and immigration policies of the host government become critical determinants of trade flows.

Table 3.2 reveals Indian IT-ITES export forecast for the period 2007-12.

Table 3.2: Indian IT-ITES Exports Forecast 2007-12

Year	IT-ITES Exports (US$ billion)
2007-08	37.6
2008-09	47.5
2009-10	60.0
2010-11	72.1
2011-12	86.6

Source: Government of India, Planning Commission, *Eleventh Five Year Plan* (2007-12), Volume III, p. 259.

In the USA and the UK the operations are facilitated by the friendlier policies on these aspects, and the EU is known to be considering the introduction of the 'blue card'–an EU-wide work permit. However, so far the immigration policies in Europe have remained problematic because of long time lines, absence of internal market mobility and non-transparent and discretionary approval processes. A similar difference has existed between the investment procedures in the USA and those in the countries on the European continent.

Table 3.3 shows the manpower requirements for IT-ITES in India

3.3 Information Technology in Indian Banking

Information technology (IT) has transformed the functioning of businesses, the world over. It has bridged the gaps in terms of the reach and the coverage of systems and enabled better decision-making based on latest and accurate information, reduced costs and overall improvement in efficiency. In the Indian context, the financial sector, especially the banking sector, has been a major beneficiary from the inroads made by IT. Many new processes, products and services offered by banks and other financial intermediaries are now IT-centred. Effective integration of technology with sound business practices requires business process re-engineering and banks in India need to follow up on the beginnings made in this regard. Newer delivery channels to customers – Automated Teller Machines (ATMs), and the networking of ATMs in the form of Shared Payment Networks, Internet Banking – and implementation of Core Banking solutions by most banks are some examples.

Table 3.3: Manpower Requirements for IT-ITES in India

	2002	2003	2006	2009	2012
IT export services					
Consulting, Integration, Installation	0.01	0.02	0.03	0.09	0.27
IT Development	0.07	0.08	0.08	0.08	0.11
Outsourced IT Support	0.09	0.11	0.17	0.28	0.53
Training and Education	0.00	0.00	0.00	0.02	0.06
Total	0.17	0.21	0.29	0.48	0.97
IT-enabled services					
Customer Care	0.03	0.05	0.15	0.42	0.03
Finance	0.02	0.03	0.05	0.09	0.21
Human Resources	0.00	0.00	0.02	0.15	0.69
Payment Services	0.00	0.1	0.05	0.14	0.45
Administration	0.2	0.3	0.5	0.15	0.15
Content Development	0.03	0.04	0.07	0.09	0.20
Total	0.11	0.16	0.38	1.0	2.72

Source: Government of India, Planning Commission, *Eleventh Five Year Plan* (2007-12), Volume III, p. 254.

The RBI has played a proactive role in the implementation of IT in the banking sector. IT based initiatives are focused on meeting the three pronged objective of better house keeping, improved customer service and overall systemic efficiency. The RBI has come out with a Financial Sector Technology Vision Document outlining the approach to be followed for IT implementation for the medium-term period of about three years. This document will help banks in finalising their IT plans in tandem with the overall approach for the banking sector, as envisioned by the RBI.

3.3.1 E-Banking: Electronic banking (E-Banking) is a generic term encompassing internet banking, telephone banking, mobile banking etc. In other words, it is a process of delivery of banking services and products through electronic channels such as telephone, internet, cell phone etc. The concept and scope of E-Banking is still evolving.

Several initiatives taken by the Government of India as well as the Reserve Bank of India (RBI) have facilitated the development of e-banking in India. As a regulator and supervisor, the RBI has made considerable progress in consolidating the existing payment and settlement systems, and in upgrading technology with a view to establishing an efficient, integrated and secure system functioning in a real-time environment, which has further helped the development of e-banking in India. The Government of India enacted the IT Act, 2000 with effect from October 17, 2000, which provides legal recognition to electronic transactions and other means of electronic commerce.

Finland was the first country in the world to have taken a lead in e-banking. The Scandinavian countries have the largest number of Internet users, with up to one-third of bank customers in Finland and Sweden taking advantage of e-banking. Internet banking is also widespread in Austria, Korea, Singapore, Spain, Switzerland, etc. E-banking facilitates an effective payment and accounting system thereby enhancing the speed of delivery of banking services considerably. While the e-banking has improved efficiency and convenience, it has also posed several challenges to the regulators and supervisors.

In response to the challenges thrown by the Internet banking, regulators and supervisors from various countries have prepared their own mechanism of regulation. There is a matrix of legislation and regulations within the United States that specifically codifies the use of and rights associated with the internet and e-commerce, in general, and electronic banking and internet banking activities, in particular. The concerns of the Federal Reserve are limited to ensuring that Internet banking and other electronic banking services are implemented with proper attention to security, safety and soundness of the bank, and the protection of the banks' customers.

In the U.K, there is no specific legislation for regulating e-banking activities. The FSA is neutral on regulations of electronic banking. In Sweden, no formal guidance has been given to examiners by the Sveriges Bank on e-banking. General guidelines apply equally to Internet banking activities. The role of the Bank of Finland has been, as part of general oversight of financial markets in Finland, mainly to monitor the ongoing development of Internet banking without active participation. The Reserve Bank of New Zealand applies the same approach to the regulation of both Internet banking activities and traditional banking activities. There are however, banking regulations that apply only to Internet banking. Supervision is based on public disclosure of information rather than application of detailed prudential rules.

The Monetary Authority of Singapore (MAS) subjects Internet banking to the same prudential standards as traditional banking. The MAS drafted an 'Internet Banking Technology Risk Management Guidelines' in September 2002, which calls upon all banks providing internet banking to establish a sound and robust risk management process. The Hong Kong regulatory approach towards e-banking is less specific in nature. The Hong Kong Monetary Authority (HKMA) expects their banks to undertake a rigorous analysis of the security aspects of their system by getting it reviewed by qualified independent experts.

Like many of these countries, India does not have specific regulatory laws for e-banking. The existing regulatory framework over banks has been extended to Internet banking as well. However, certain guidelines have been issued to banks to recognise the risks arising from electronic modes and to devise control mechanisms that are needed to mitigate such risks. Banks offering the e-banking services in India need to comply with the guidelines.

The RBI has been gearing up to upgrading itself as a regulator and supervisor of the technologically dominated financial system. In 1998, it availed the technical assistance project of Department for International Development (DFID), UK for upgrading its supervisory system and adaptation of its supervisory functions to the computerised environment. It issued guidelines on 'risks and control in computer and telecommunication system' in February 1998 to all the banks advising them to evaluate the risks inherent in the systems and put in place adequate control mechanisms to address these risks, which can be broadly put under three heads, viz., IT environment risks, IT operations risks and product risks.

The existing regulatory framework over banks has also been extended to internet banking. These guidelines cover various issues that would fall within the framework of technology, security standards and legal and regulatory issues. Virtual banks, which have no offices and function only on line are not permitted to offer e-banking services in India and that only banks licensed under the Banking Regulation Act and having a physical presence in India are allowed to offer such services. Further, banks are required to report to the RBI every breach or failure of security systems and procedures in Internet banking, while the RBI at its discretion may decide to commission special audit/inspection of such banks.

As per recent guidelines, banks no longer need any prior approval of the Reserve Bank for offering the internet banking services. Nevertheless, banks must have their internet policy and they need to ensure that it is in line with parameters as set by the Working Group on Internet Banking in India (2001).

E-banking is based on technology that by its very nature is designed to expand the "virtual" geographic reach of banks and customers without necessarily requiring a similar "physical" expansion. Such market expansion can extend beyond national borders which significantly increases cross-border cooperation challenges for bank supervisors due to the following factors.

- The potential ease and speed with which banks located anywhere in the world can conduct activities with customers over interconnected electronic networks into countries where a bank is not licensed or supervised.
- The potential ability of a bank or non-bank to use the Internet to cross borders and to seamlessly link banking activities that have typically been subject to supervision with non-banking activities that might be unsupervised by any financial market authority.
- The practical difficulties faced by national authorities wishing to monitor or control local access to e-banking sites originating in other jurisdictions without the cooperation of home country authorities.

Banking organisations have been delivering services to consumers and businesses remotely for years. Electronic funds transfer, including small payments and corporate cash management systems, as well as publicly accessible machines for currency withdrawal and retail account management are global fixtures. However, delivering financial services over public networks such as the Internet is bringing about a fundamental shift in the financial services industry.

The changes created, and some of the technical characteristics of internet technology raise new concerns for both bankers and supervisors. Banking organisations are focusing increasingly on their e-banking activities and are globally expanding Internet banking activities, exploring the use of wireless networks and venturing into some new areas of electronic commerce.

Banks offer e-banking services to defend or expand market share or as a cost saving strategy to reduce paperwork and personnel. The Internet also provides banks with substantial opportunity to extend their customer reach beyond existing boundaries. However, the nature of the open network and the evolution of electronic commerce exposes banks to significant competition from both banking and non-banking firms. In addition, electronic delivery channels operate in an uncertain legal and regulatory environment that differs by jurisdiction.

All these factors present new challenges for financial institutions in managing security, integrity and availability of services provided while remaining sufficiently profitable.

Following are the emerging trends and issues that could impact bank risk profiles.

- A significant increase in competition in the electronic financial services industry as both banking and non-banking firms rapidly introduce new financial products and services.
- Rapid technological improvements in telecommunications and computer hardware and software enabling greater speed in transactions processing.
- Bank management and staff often lack expertise in technology and e-banking risk issues.
- Greater reliance on outsourcing to third party service providers, and a proliferation of new alliances and joint ventures with non-financial firms.
- Greater demand for global infrastructures for technology that are scalable, flexible and interoperable, both within and across enterprises and that can ensure the security, integrity and availability of information and services.
- Increased potential for fraud, due to the absence of standard business practices for customer verification and authentication on open networks like the Internet.
- Legal and regulatory ambiguity and uncertainty with respect to the application and jurisdiction of current laws and regulations to evolving e-banking activities.
- The collection, storage and frequent sharing of significant quantities of customer data can lead to customer privacy issues that potentially create prudential risks for banks

(e.g. legal and reputational).

- Questions regarding the effectiveness and efficiency of online disclosures. Lengthy or complicated online disclosures may cause customers to simply "click through" or even quit a web site; moreover, extensive disclosure reduces the speed at which web sites and pages can be downloaded.

Banks and bank supervisors generally agree that the supervisory principles that apply to traditional banking are applicable to e-banking. However, the combination of rapid changes in technology and the degree of bank dependence on technology vendors and service providers modify and sometimes magnify traditional risks. Hence, there is a need for additional supervisory guidance in selected areas to enhance the overall risk management framework for e-banking activities.

These developments in e-banking to date suggest the following.

- The desire to benefit from the advantages of e-commerce in financial services has become widespread. The financial services industry is increasingly focused on providing technology-based financial services solutions directly to customers in order to help build and retain customer bases.
- Speed-to-market has become a critical factor for success in e-banking. To reduce time to market, banking institutions are allying with non-banking firms to provide total financial services solutions.
- The current trends in the formation of strategic alliances and technology outsourcing will grow.

These developments present challenges for both banks and bank supervisors. Bank management needs to re-evaluate the robustness of traditional risk management practices in light of the new risks posed by e-banking activities. Also, bank supervisors need to take a balanced approach to the introduction of new regulation and supervisory policy on e-banking, so as to ensure safe and sound operations of banks while at the same time not stifling innovation and the competitiveness of the banks relative to non-banks.

3.3.2 Electronic Money (E-Money): In recent years, there has been a gradual switchover from the use of paper-based payments media to those based on electronics. While the basic characteristics of these new instruments are by and large similar to those of paper-based instruments, the former present a different set of challenges to policy makers. Electronic money (e-money) is one such new product which has appeared on Indian horizon recently.

E-money may be broadly defined as an electronic store of monetary value on a technical device used for making payments to undertakings other than the issuer without necessarily involving bank accounts in the transaction, but acting as a prepaid bearer instrument. These products could be classified into two broad categories, viz. (a) pre-paid stored value card (sometimes called "electronic purse") and (b) pre-paid software based product that uses computer networks such as internet (sometimes referred to as "digital cash" or "network money"). The stored value card scheme typically uses a microprocessor chip embedded in a plastic card while software based scheme typically uses specialized software installed in a personal computer.

In January 2002, the RBI constituted a Working Group on Electronic Money which submitted its report in July 2002. The Group identified certain areas of concern from the point of view of the central bank in the context of more widespread use of e-money so that the conduct of monetary policy is not impaired and at the same time, the integrity of the instrument is also preserved. Some of the suggestions made by the Group included (a) multi-purpose e-money to be issued only by authorized banks on a credit basis, which should be strictly regulated and closely monitored, (b) ensure redeem ability in order to preserve the unit of account function of money as well as to control money supply in the economy and (c) reporting of monetary statistics for the purposes of monetary policy and protection against criminal abuse, such as money laundering.

Summary and recommendations of the Report are set forth below.

Broadly, e-money is an electronic store of monetary value on a technical device. E-money could be classified as (a) pre-paid stored value card (sometimes called "electronic purse") and (b) pre-paid software based product that uses computer networks such as internet (sometimes referred to as "digital cash" or "network money"). The stored value card could be of three types - single-purpose card, closed-system or limited-purpose card and general-purpose or multi-purpose card. The single-purpose card generally with a magnetic chip recording the amount of fund therein is designed to facilitate only one type of transaction e.g., telephone calls, public transportation, laundry, parking facilities etc. Here, the distinguishing point is that the issuer and the service provider (acceptor) are identical for such cards. The closed-system or the limited-purpose cards are generally used in a small number of well-identified points of sale within a well-identified location such as corporate/university campus. The multi-purpose card on the other can perform variety of functions with several vendors viz., credit card, debit card, stored value card, identification card, repository of personal medical information etc.

While it may not be desirable place any limit on storing monetary value in e-money, it is expected that e-money could be used to substitute central bank notes and coins at least partially. However, the importance of e-money with respect to regulatory oversight, restrictions on issuers and their implications for monetary policy is extremely critical from the point of view of the central bank.

After considering various issues, the Group recommends that multi-purpose e-money may be permitted to be issued only against payment of full value of central bank money or against credit only by the banks. The issuance of e-money on credit basis should, however, be strictly regulated and closely monitored.

It needs to be appreciated that issuers must be under obligation to offer redemption of their e-money liabilities net of service charges, if so required. From monetary policy point of view, such redemption requirement is essential in order to preserve unit of account function of money as also to control money supply in the economy.

With regard to status of issuers of e-money, it may be indicated that there are five reasons which may warrant banks as the issuers of multi-purpose e-money. These include attributes of e-money being closure to demand liabilities of the bank, implications of e-money on velocity of circulation of money and its corresponding impact on monetary statistics, the option to impose reserve requirement on e-money, the need for closure monitoring of e-money when these would be issued as credit and the technical security of e-money. For all these reasons, the Group recommends that only banks should be allowed to issue multi-purpose e-money. However, single-purpose and limited-purpose e-money should be allowed to be issued by any entity including banks.

Non-banks should not be permitted to issue multi-purpose e-money. If they are permitted, they along with banks must conform to seven minimum prudential requirements as laid down by European Central Bank (ECB) in 1998. These are (i) prudential supervision of issuers of e-money by the central bank, (ii) solid and transparent legal arrangements codifying the rights and obligations of issuers, merchants, consumers and the regulators, (iii) adequate technical, organizational and procedural safeguards to prevent and detect threats to the security of e-money, (iv) protection against criminal abuse, (v) supplying of all relevant information to the central bank for the purpose of monetary policy, (vi) legal obligations to redeem e-money against central bank money at par at the request of the holder and (vii) the right of the central bank to impose reserve requirement on issuers of e-money.

E-money could have profound impact on compilation of monetary statistics and money supply unless regulated prudently. E-money could be issued against cash (i.e., 100 per cent backed by central bank money paid upfront). Since e-money are close substitutes of central bank money, these should be explicitly accounted for in monetary statistics. If e-money is allowed to be issued only by banks, then currency would be substituted with demand/time liabilities through e-money. In that eventually, issuance of e-money would be money stock neutral and no change would be required in the definition of money stock. However, if e-money is issued by entities other than depository institutions (i.e., banks), the money creating sector as embedded in compilation of monetary statistics would need to be broadened.

There could be a situation where residents could use e-money supplied by entities outside the country for domestic transactions. In that case, monetary aggregates would lose its predictive power.

It is expected that the proportion of interest bearing liabilities in monetary aggregates would grow in the event of growing use of e-money which would render them more unstable, and information content of monetary aggregates would also change.

If e-money is issued on credit, there is a possibility that the issuers may assume a leveraged position. There is, therefore, a need for continuous monitoring of the behaviour of issuing authorities for balanced growth of their assets and liabilities, particularly liabilities arising out of issuance of e-money. For these reasons, the Group recommends that the central bank should regulate and closely monitor the practice of issuing e-money on credit.

If consumers prefer to use e-money vis-à-vis currency, then for a given stock of currency, the money multiplier would go up which would in turn increase the aggregate money supply in the economy more than what would have been the case without e-money. Also, with large scale use of e-money, it has been apprehended that central bank's balance sheet may shrink to such an extent relative to that of the banking sector that it may be unable to perform its liquidity absorption function on account of non-availability of adequate volume of assets. Apart from constraining its liquidity management function, relative shrinkage in balance sheet may also have serious implications regarding loss of seigniorage revenue for the central bank. As a counter argument, it is maintained that there should always be a lower bound below which the use of currency notes and coins should not go down so that there should also be a limit below which reserve money should not shrink relative to broad money stock.

A review of developments indicate that while considerations of potential benefits of micro-economic efficiency, extension of banking to urban poor and rural communities and facilitation of e-governance demand that there should be increasingly private provision of payment and settlement services in the economy in future, macro-economic stabilisation policy warrants that there should be a case for public regulation over such provision. Also, currency uses are characterised by network externalities in that larger the number of users, larger is the settlement value of the currency concerned implying that currency could at best be supplied oligopolistically. There are, in fact, the fundamental reasons for which the "monopoly right" in the issuance of currency should be in the hands of some public authority, preferably the central bank. Even then, there cannot be any final judgement on this issue at this point of time. In view of all these considerations, the Group, therefore, recommends that the RBI should regularly monitor closely all these developments so that integrity of the financial system is preserved.

The RBI should also periodically review issues relating to legal framework, if any, technical security and the clearing and settlement arrangements of different e-money schemes and the practices of various e-money schemes, both in India and abroad, for preserving integrity of the financial market. On the issue whether entities other than the central bank could issue independent media of exchanges, the Group feels that such a possibility is apparently remote in India at this point of time. However, RBI may continually keep track of these developments for smooth functioning of the financial market.

No innovation is without challenges and IT is no exception to this rule. The most prominent challenge arising from these innovations relates to the concept of security. Considering the scope for fraud in the e-banking area and the possibility of contagion, the Reserve Bank as a regulator and supervisor has been proactive in addressing the risks associated with e-banking that could have otherwise undermined the credibility of the Indian banking sector. The Reserve Bank has been promptly addressing issues related to fraud with the use of electronic banking facility. Even after issuing guidelines for a secured e-banking, the Reserve Bank from time to time advises the banks on control mechanisms to combat such frauds. In a recent case of attempt of fraud by a customer while using internet banking facility, the Reserve Bank advised the concerned bank to plug the loopholes and the same was also communicated to other banks so that they remained vigilant and control the misuse of internet banking system.

In India, the legal infrastructure for promoting e-banking has not yet been put in place in a comprehensive manner. India does not have a licensed certifying authority appointed by the Controller of Certifying Authorities to issue digital signature certificates. Also, India is not yet a signatory to the International Cyber Crime Treaty, which seeks to intensify co-operation among different signatory nations for exchanging information concerning crime and cyber criminals. Further, there are unresolved legislative issues related to cyber crimes laws, clarification relating to regulatory authority over e-money products, consumer protection and privacy laws. To make the e-banking operations in India more widespread, secure and efficient, these issues need to be addressed by relevant authorities.

As the banking practices and legislations concerning e-banking are still in the process of evolution in India and abroad because of technological innovations, there is a need for a constant review of various legislations and regulatory framework relating to banking and commerce. The Reserve Bank is monitoring and reviewing the legal and other requirements of e-banking on a continuous basis to ensure that the e-banking would develop on sound lines and the e-banking related challenges would not pose a threat to financial stability.

3.4 Information Technology in Agriculture

The rapid strides that the country has registered in the IT field will remain incomplete unless IT is fully utilised to ensure more efficient and productive Indian agriculture. Practically there is no area in agriculture in which IT has no role to play. The immense scale and diversity of Indian agriculture provides the ultimate challenge to the potential of information technology.

The adoption of IT services in agriculture depends on the main functionaries involved in Indian agriculture. These functionaries can make a big contribution to the growth of agriculture with the assistance of IT. For this purpose, the following functionaries can be considered (a) farmers, (b) industries providing inputs to agriculture, (c) industries dealing with agricultural output, (d) central and state governments and (e) NGOs working for the benefit of farmers and agricultural universities and research centres.

Indian farmers, for whose welfare a huge government machinery is devoted, still suffer from the absence of right information at the required time. The farmers require timely information on weather conditions, sowing time, availability of inputs including credit, expert advice on maintaining his crop in healthy condition, information on markets and on all other areas of interest to him and his family.

In spite of the best efforts and expenditure, the conventional apparatus has not been able to deliver the goods satisfactorily. Herein lies the role of IT which can efficiently address the concerns of farmers stationed at even remote locations. Low literacy levels, cost of computers, poor communication infrastructure make it impossible for individual farmers, particularly small farmers, to directly adopt IT. This calls for institutional efforts to provide IT-based services to farmers.

In order to keep pace with the state-of-the-art technologies, NIC has been conducting various training programmes on IT application on a regular basis from time to time for the user organizations of agriculture sector.

Agricultural Informatics Division of NIC has taken up various initiatives in bringing IT led development which includes Web enabled applications, GIS based applications, Multimedia applications, Database applications and e-Governance and training etc., in the Ministry of Agriculture.

Recently, IFFCO has initiated IT-based services for farmers and cooperative societies. It has taken up a project in association with Indian Space Research Organisation (ISRO) to utilise satellite based remote sensing data and Geographical Information Systems (GIS). Developed countries have been utilising precision farming with the help of IT tools for a long time. While this will take a long time for our country due to small holdings, it is to be noted that GIS has an invaluable role to play even in the existing conditions. Remote sensing and GIS information can provide warnings on evolving crop stresses, crop vigour etc.

The IFFCO-ISRO GIS project extends support for efficient and timely availability of IFFCO's fertiliser to farmers though better logistics and efficient operations. Based on the experience gained from this project, more intensive services based on GIS are envisaged for the entire country. In addition to the GIS-based services, effort is being made to create databases that contain information of interest to the farmers. These include recommendation on package of practices for major cereals, pulses, horticulture, floriculture and animal husbandry etc. Information on various inputs such as seeds, fertilisers, credit is provided. An important service envisaged is to provide access to the nearest expert in case of stress or any other problem witnessed in the crops. Facilities are sought to be provided to encourage and share farm experiences by forging various crop forums. Many of the agricultural extension services are also proposed to be made online using multimedia facilities.

In order to encourage farmers to obtain best possible price, information regarding prices of various crops prevailing in approachable markets (mandies) is also being provided. Other areas of interest to farmers such as distance education, location specific news etc. are also planned.

To take IT to the door steps of the farmers, it is proposed that a large number of access points called cyber dhabas are setup. These cyber dhabas should be provided with a PC and a modem with telephone connection to connect to the databases. The farmers can take the assistance of the operator of cyber dhabas for a nominal charge.

The major bottleneck in spreading e-culture to rural areas is related to connectivity i.e. ensuring that the access points can get connected to the databases which are in selected locations. Since dialup lines are very slow, other viable options are required to be explored. Unfortunately, the alternatives are expensive and may not be feasible. One silver lining is that several private operators are connecting important cities with fiber optic which provides a very reliable and fast access. Since these will pass through rural areas, it is possible to explore the possibility of tapping this potential by laying the last mile connectivity. Once this is done, substantial segment of rural India can access the IT-based services.

E-Choupal, ITC's unique web-based initiative, offers farmers the information, products and services they need to enhance productivity, improve farm-gate price realisation, and cut transaction costs. Farmers can access the latest local and global information on weather, scientific farming practices, as well as market prices at the village itself through this web portal-all in Hindi. E-Choupal also facilitates the supply of high quality farm inputs as well as the purchase of commodities at the farm.

Given the literacy and infrastructure constraints at the village level, this model is designed to provide physical service support through a choupal sanchalak, himself a lead farmer, who acts as the interface between the system and the farmers. The contents of this site in their entirety are made available only to the registered sanchalaks.

The National E-governance Plan (2003-07) reflects the strategic intent of the central government in the right perspective. Many projects are earmarked under this plan, and it is trying to address the digital divide.

From a political perspective, after watching the performance of some IT-savvy states in the recent elections, the system has woken up to the need to focus more on rural development. The political systems are keener to use IT to disseminate information faster to farmers, disburse loans, improve education and the health systems in villages etc. There is a clear-cut incentive to do it as 60 percent of the vote-bank still lives in rural India.

E-governance has to be supported by the will and resources of those who are in governance, be it at the central or state level. The central government has analyzed and appreciated the concept by creating a separate E-governance department headed by a secretary to trigger e-governance in India. The World Bank, ADB and UN have been approached, and in response they are generously funding e-governance projects. In future, education, agriculture, state wide area networks (SWANs) and Community Information Centre projects will be rolled out backed by a strong public private participation model (PPP) to achieve long-term sustainability. Projects with PPP models in these segments can revolutionize the governance experience.

Proper planning,.monitoring and corrective action requires availability of timely information of right quality. The Central and State Governments require to hasten the process of computerisation of all the records and transactions. Since the government has a major say in promoting agriculture, this will have cascading effect on the entire rural areas. To begin with, it is necessary that the government agencies should accept conventional reports in the electronic format. This will bring about much desired speed and effectiveness in governance. Many State Governments are showing interest in developing proper systems for e-governance. But the implementation of the same is still requires a lot to be desired. The Central and State Governments should also make information available for ready reference by those interested. This will be not only helpful to people but also will raise interest levels in IT-based services. Similarly, research institutions and NGOs should exchange and provide information through a well conceived network. These measures will encourage end user, i.e. Farmer's participation and will provide the much needed input from them.

The face of the Indian agriculture can be transformed by a well conceived deployment of IT. The potential of IT as yet remains untapped and urgent measures are required to derive maximum benefit. The key players involved in this process such as industry, government and educational institutions and research centres are required to make contributions in this endeavour. The initiative to develop necessary IT-based agricultural services need to be developed immediately. Parallel steps to develop necessary IT communication infrastructure are to be taken up along with the utilisation of fiber optic network wherever it is passing through the rural segments.

The Karnataka Government's Bhoomi project has led to the computerisation of the centuries-old system of handwritten rural land records. Through it, the revenue department has done away with the corruption-ridden system that involved bribing village accountants to procure land records; records of right, tenancy and cultivation certificates. The project is expected to benefit seventy lakh villagers in 30,000 villages.
A farmer can walk into the nearest taluk office and ask for a

computer printout of his land record certificate for Rs. 15. He can also check details of land records on a touch-screen kiosk by inserting a two-rupee coin. These kiosks, installed at the taluk office, will provide the public with a convenient interface to the land records centre.

3.5 Challenges Facing Indian IT and IT-enabled Services

Abundant talent available at lower cost, quality infrastructure in Indian cities, government incentives and growing domestic IT/BPO market are among the reasons, which have contributed to India being able to strengthen its leadership position. The industry attributes the success of Indian IT and BPO also to the support provided by the Government of India and individual State Governments through an enabling business policy and regulatory environment as well as information security provided by means of Indian laws and by voluntary action by industry associations. Recent analyses by experts have revealed that the above sources of strength are getting eroded and the industry is likely to face several challenges in future. In order to consider what further needs to be done by the Central and State governments to sustain and enhance India's competitiveness the Group examined the evolving situation on each of the elements that have constituted a source of strength of industry so far.

The most important physical infrastructure needs of IT and BPO are power and telecommunications, but there is significant dependence on urban infrastructure including road transport as well. The personnel need to move speedily from their homes to workplace and they require good urban infrastructure for providing them with quality of life. Proximity to airports and good international air connections are also critical to enable them to travel frequently to foreign destinations. With all these facilities the industry requires office space. Big players need developed land to construct their own buildings but others need rented accommodation provided by developers in which they can move quickly.

Developments following the end of Government of India monopoly in public telecommunications resulting in large capacity creation by the private sector and significant decline in tariffs coupled with improvement in service quality have been one of the factors contributing to the growth of IT and BPO. Large capacity expansion by a number of players has established a strong framework of planned redundancies, thus ensuring continuous network connectivity. Telecom is one infrastructure service in which no impediment is foreseen in the expansion of IT and BPO services. There is only a data protection related handicap created by restrictions in connectivity of home telephones, which inhibits the qualified homemakers from joining the workforce in their spare time.

One of the key requirements for the competitiveness of the Indian IT and BPO industry is assurance of information security, which is a sensitive concern of all customers. By virtue of its adherence to the WTO TRIPS Agreement India is committed to the introduction of world class intellectual property laws and it is widely recognised that these laws are now in position. Of particular relevance to the IT and BPO sector are the Indian Copyright Act, as under the Indian law computer programmes have copyright protection, not patent protection. While the law is considered adequate, it is the area of enforcement that needs considerable improvement. Conviction percentage is low, cases take a long time to get decided and the organised nature of piracy is not addressed in the enforcement strategy. The awareness of the criminal justice system needs to be raised, followed by skill development, process standardisation and use of scientific evidence.

The Information Technology Act, 2000 provides inter alia for data protection and privacy of information held in the computer systems or networks. Section 43 provides for civil liability to pay damages if a person accesses data stored in a computer system without authorisation. Section 66 provides for prosecution of a person who commits hacking of a computer system and section 72 provides for penalties for breach of confidentiality and privacy by a person, who having secured the data lawfully discloses the data without consent of the person concerned. These specific laws are supported by the provisions in the general laws of the country, including the Indian Contract Act and the Indian Penal Code. Most urban police units in the country have acquired the basic understanding of cyber crimes, but need to progress to the next level, of acquiring specialised forensic equipment and using it to solve more complicated cases.

There can be no doubt that after the economic reforms of 1991-92, liberalisation of external trade, elimination of duties on imports of information technology products, relaxation of controls on both inward and outward investments and foreign exchange and the fiscal measures taken by the Government of India and the State Governments and other incentives provided by them specifically for IT and BPO services have been major contributory factors for the sector to flourish in India and for the country to be able to acquire a dominant position in offshored services in the world. The major fiscal incentives provided by the Government of India have been for the Export Oriented Units (EOU), Software Technology Parks (STP), Special Economic Zones (SEZ) and Electronic Hardware Technology Park (EHTP). Some of the other benefits available to the sector are the EPCG scheme, the Star Export House Scheme & Target Plus Scheme, Services Tax Exemptions and certain specific customs and excise duty exemptions for inputs and specified capital goods for IT hardware and software.

One of the most effective schemes for the promotion of exports of IT and BPO is the Software Technology Parks of India (STPI) programme. The 48 STPIs that have been set up since inception of the programme have given a major boost to IT and BPO services exports. Apart from exemption from customs duty available for capital goods (with a few exemptions) there are also exemptions from service tax, excise duty, and rebate for payment of Central Sales Tax. But the most important incentive available is 100 per cent exemption from Income Tax of export profits for a period of 10 year beginning from the commencement of manufacturing. However, the exemption for export profits is due to expire on March 31, 2009. SEZ Act 2005 gives benefits to units within the SEZ in respect of exports similar to those available to units within STPIs in respect of indirect taxes, although there are minor differences in operational details. There is a significant difference, however, in respect of income tax holiday: in that the exemption from income tax is tapered down over 15 years from the date of commencement of manufacture. There is 100 per cent exemption of export profits from income tax for the first five years, 50 per cent for the next five years and 50 per cent for the another five years subject to transfer of profits to special reserves.

But the most important difference is that unlike in the STPI there is no overriding sunset clause and new SEZ units will go on getting the benefits for a period of 15 years from the commencement of manufacturing for each of them. With the sunset clause for income tax exemption for STPIs becoming effective on March 31, 2009, there is a major problem of non-level playing field between units within existing STPIs and new units set up in the SEZs. Those within STPIs will stop getting income tax exemption and those within SEZs will be getting benefits for 15 years from the date of commencement of manufacturing. The STPIs are particularly concerned because their income tax benefits are coming to an end at a time when their profits have shrunk because of the appreciation of the Indian Rupee.

4

Retail Trading Services

4.1 Introduction

Indian retail business is undergoing dramatic transformation. The retail sector employs about 8 per cent of the country's workforce and is characterised by a high degree of fragmentation with over 5 million outlets. Due to their small size, Indian retailers have very little bargaining power vis-à-vis manufacturers unlike in the case of retailers in developed countries.

The corner grocer or the kirana store is a key element in the retail business in India due to the housewife's unwillingness to go long distances for purchasing daily needs. In the emerging scenario, traditional formats of retailing (like hawkers, grocers and paan shops) are now co-existing with modern formats like supermarkets and non-store retailing channels such as multi-level marketing and teleshopping.

Retailing has been defined as a business activity involving sale of goods and services to consumers for their personal, family or household use. Although retailing has been around since times immemorial, it was in the 20th century that significant changes occurred in the retail sector, especially in the developed countries. Modern formats of retailing, such as department stores, discount stores, supermarkets, convenience stores, fast food outlets, specialty stores, warehouse retailers and hypermarkets, are now making inroads into developing countries of the world. Retailing has become more organised and chain stores (using sophisticated information technology and communication to manage their operations) are coming up at the expense of independent shops.

The emergence of new formats of retailing has attracted the attention of government functionaries, company managers, economic analysts and the public at large.

Modern stores tend to be larger, carry more stock and have a self-service format. Modern formats also tend to have higher levels of sales per unit of space, stock turnover and gross margin but lower levels of net margin as compared to traditional formats. Modernisation in retail formats is likely to happen quicker in categories like dry groceries, electronics, men's apparel, books and music. Some reshaping and adaptation my also happen in fresh groceries, women's apparel, fast food, and personal care products.

At present the new format stores cater mostly to households belonging to the higher income families. The catchments area for these modern stores has to be fairly large as the number of such households is small in relation to the total population.

Manufacturing firms will need to develop new strategies for dealing with powerful retailers. The first change required will be one of mind-set. Negotiations with powerful retailers will have to be carried out at much higher executive levels within the firm. New structures such as national account managers and category managers would need to be deployed. Firms will have to reconsider their brand promise, brand promotion and their brand building policies to deal with store brands that will be introduced by retail chains. Firms will also have to re-engineer their logistic policies to meet the demands of powerful retailers for in-time delivery to their distribution centres/stores. New product introductions will have to be coordinated with the retail chains so that adequate shelf space is available at the time of launch. The firms will need to carefully look at their product cost structures both in terms of variable cost and fixed costs in order to maintain profitability in the face of pressure for price reductions from powerful retailers.

The Indian retail sector is largely traditional, but stores in modern format are emerging. The contribution of organised retailing in the share of retail sales in India is currently very small. Based on the experience of retail developments in countries like Thailand, Brazil and Greece, it is possible to conclude that modernisation of retailing in India is round the corner. The development of modern retail system will have several implications for managerial practices in manufacturing firms. Firms will have to proactively review their sales structures, brand activities, logistics policy and price structure to cope with pressures from powerful retailers.

The structure of a country's retail sector has an enormous influence on marketing strategy and marketing activities of firms. The Indian retail sector has arrived at a very critical stage. Stores in modern formats have emerged in the metropolitan cities but the bulk of the retail sales still take place through traditional retail formats. The development of modern retailing is of great interest to marketing scholars, practitioners and policy makers.

4.2 Indian Retail Sector

Retailing in India is largely unorganized, dominated by the kirana shops or groceries in every locality, supplemented by paan & beedi shops, handcart or head load hawkers and pavement vendors. The urban areas also have owner-manned general stores and specialty stores, the most common being those dealing with apparel, footwear, drugs and medicines. Until a few years back, organized retailing was uncommon, although the States in the South have had a few small retail chains for decades. However, recent years have witnessed considerable activity by the organized sector and several corporate-backed retail chains have come to the fore and are opening large numbers of stores all over the country. What has helped this trend is the rapid growth of the upper middle class, with increasing disposable incomes, and working couples, who have less time for daily shopping of groceries. Even so, organized retail is in its infancy in India and its share in 2006 is estimated to be only 4% of the retail sales in the country. As against this the share of organized retail in United Kingdom,

Germany and France in that year was 80 per cent and in the USA it was 85 per cent. Even in emerging economies the percentage share of organized retail was considerably higher than in India: Brazil (36); China (20); Indonesia (30); Korea (15) and Malaysia (55).

Organized retail has so far been concentrated in the clothing and footwear, with furniture, furnishing, appliances and services in the second position. Food & grocery retailing by the organized sector is less than one per cent of the total retail turnover. It may be observed however that some large retail chains, which have entered the scene lately, would be dealing with grocery as well.

4.3 Foreign Direct Investment in Retailing

After the introduction of economic reforms in 1991-92 foreign direct investment was gradually liberalized in both manufacturing and services sectors, starting with permission given on a case-by-case basis. At that time one or two foreign companies were given permission to do retail business in the country. However, the position changed in 1997, and contrary to the general direction of reform FDI in retail was prohibited on fears that entry of foreign retail companies would have an unfavourable impact on the unorganized sector and would lead to the outflow of foreign exchange. Since then the policy has been relaxed partially and in 2006 foreign companies were allowed to invest up to 51% equity in single-brand retail joint ventures.

FDI in multi-brand retailing is still prohibited. However, the point is made that FDI has made inroads into retailing through several routes. 100 per cent equity is allowed for cash-and carry wholesale trading but there is no dividing line between this activity and retail trading. There is nothing to prevent the end-use consumers to make wholesale purchases meant for their own consumption. Inroads into activity in the domestic economy have also been made by foreign enterprises through franchising, which is permitted. Further the following types of trading, which is permitted partake of the nature of retail activity:

- Trading of hi-tech items requiring specialized after-sale service
- Trading of items for social sector
- Trading of high-tech medical and diagnostic items
- Test marketing for a period of two years for items for which a company has approval for manufacturing

Even so retailing is the only large service sector, which has not been formally opened to FDI in a big way. Since some policy makers want to maintain the momentum of liberalization many of them feel that there should be some more movement toward liberalization. Among the gains that they visualize are the technology and know how coming into the country with the large retail chains. The backward linkages developed by the large retailing organizations are likely to help in the scientific development of farming. The case is cited of Macdonald's, which has invested in setting up of supply chains and transferred state-of-the-art food processing technology. Macdonald and its suppliers also worked closely with farmers in some locations in the country to cultivate high quality lettuce. The most significant point that is made is that once the foreign retail chains develop local supplies up to their standard for the local operations, they can also source the same products for the operations in home country as well as in third countries. The activities of the large retail organizations can thus become a big avenue for increasing exports from the country. However, these arguments have not been enough to convince the opponents of FDI in retail and there is lack of consensus on the issue in the ruling coalition.

4.4 Organized versus Unorganized Retailing

As a result of the entry of large business houses into retailing and ambitious plans being implemented by them, the FDI issue has receded into the background somewhat. The small retailers now feel threatened by the organized retail giants, and there have been demonstrations in West Bengal and Jharkhand by vegetable vendors. The State Government of Uttar Pradesh has taken pre-emptive action by shutting down independent outlets of retail chains dealing with fresh farm products. The big issue now is whether organized retailing would throw the unorganized sector out of business. One view expressed on this is that local kirana shops and established vegetable vendors would retain their position as convenience shops and would not be displaced. Another view is that since the economy is rising at a rapid pace organized sector will take care of the resultant expansion of retailing activity, leaving the present position of unorganized retail secure to a large extent. It is true that at the height of Asian financial crisis foreign retailers were allowed entry by Thailand the local players were marginalized.

However, in India this is not likely to happen in the present times when the economy is expanding rapidly. Most people believe that the organized sector will see new jobs of a higher quality than the organized and there would more jobs for the educated and skilled categories. Nagging doubts remain, however, in some sections about the possibility of adverse effect on the self-employed people in the unorganized retail sector especially if the organized sector expands too fast. Others point out that the benefit to consumers by way of economy in purchases and multiple choice and the benefit to the government by way of increased collection of taxes would far outweigh the adverse effect if any on the small retailers.

4.5 Challenges Facing Organized Retail Sector

Retail trade depends critically on the quality of physical infrastructure, particularly on power and roads. The shortcomings of the power sector in the country are well known. Retail trade is significantly dependent on supply of electricity for lighting as well as for refrigeration and deficiencies in the quality and quantity of supplies impairs its efficiency. The need to maintain captive power plants on a standby increases the fixed cost and if the outages from the main grid are for long periods the high cost of generation in small plants increases the variable cost as well. The cost of generation of small captive units is as much as four times that of supplies from the grid.

The world over supplies for retailers, whether of fresh or manufactured goods move by roads, sometimes over long distances. While the National Highways programme has made has made good progress the traffic constraint problems e.g. mix of motorized and non-motorized traffic, ribbon development, check-posts on interstate borders by various State authorities. The cumulative result of all this is that vehicles move at very slow speed. Delhi-Mumbai takes three days and Delhi-Bangalore five days, when by international standards they should not be taking more than two or three days respectively. The poor road transportation infrastructure is compounded by the lack of penetration of information technology in the transport sector and by the lack of proper communications infrastructure. In the absence of a shipment tracking system a shipper cannot track the status of a shipment before it reaches the destination.

The longer time involved in road transportation and the absence of a proper communications infrastructure increases the cost of transport and consequently the logistical cost. Retail trade is heavily dependent on logistics and increases in logistical cost impair the efficiency of retail trade.

Urban infrastructure, and particularly urban transport infrastructure, is also critical for retail trade. The goods that are brought in from outside for the retail outlets have to be moved into these towns and cities through congested streets, on which the larger vehicles used for trunk routes cannot move.

For maximum benefit to the consumer the retail trade chains must operate in several States or preferably on a pan-India basis. Any tax on interstate movement such as the Central Sales Tax constrains retail operations as the supplies have to be sourced within the State to avoid the tax.

Differences in the levels of State taxes also lead to the same results and the retail chains are unable to avail of economies of scale that could be reaped from the centralized procurement of merchandise. Similarly the benefit of backward supply linkages developed in one State gets circumscribed to that State. Octroi or entry taxes levied by the municipal bodies exacerbate the position. Differences in the level of taxes also impost costs on retail operations as the goods have to be priced differentially in various State jurisdictions.

Fortunately the fiscal reforms introduced in recent years are likely to ease the situation in the near future. Phase-out of the Central Sales Tax has commenced and there will be no tax on interstate movement with effect from 31 March 2010. State VAT was introduced by most States with effect from 1 April 2005 and other States have been gradually falling in line. After the decision made lately by Uttar Pradesh all States have agreed to introduce State VAT. This will bring in uniformity in internal taxation of most goods in the country and facilitate retail operations. The Government of Maharashtra has recently decided to withdraw octroi in Mumbai.

The decision in principle to introduce Goods and Services Tax (GST) on 1 April 2010 to integrate all indirect taxes on goods and services at the central and state levels is another positive development for retail trade. A dual tax structure, one at the state level and the other at the central level is likely to be established at the beginning of the financial year 2010-11. The eventual establishment of GST would lead to a quantum improvement in the efficiency of the retail sector

4.5.1 Supply Chains: The world over food and grocery items including fresh fruits and vegetables constitute the largest segment of retail trade. In India retail operations are handicapped by the presence of multiple levels of intermediaries in distribution of these items. The Agricultural Produce Marketing Committee (APMC) Act, which was originally enacted to assist the farmers in getting the best price for their produce became an impediment in achieving this objective as it trapped them in the stranglehold of arhatias (wholesalers). Further one of the advantages of modern retail industry is that the farmers supplying the produce are provided with technology to improve their farming practices as a result of which the retailers have better produce on their shelves and the farmers increase their incomes. For this to become possible the farmers have to undertake contract farming and sell their products directly to the retail chains. The APMC Act bars such an arrangement, as the farm produce must be sold in the designated markets. While many States have amended their laws and eliminated the obstacle in the way of contract farming the process is still hampered in the absence of a specific law on contract farming affording speedy relief against violations of contract farming.

For efficient operations the retail chains need logistic service providers, to whom a company's entire logistic operations can be outsourced. The logistics industry in India is highly fragmented with each of the segments, road transportation, freight forwarding, warehousing, and management of information service dominated by small operators. Few of the service providers have the capability of providing service in more than one segment and Third Party Logistics (3PL) companies with the capability of providing multiple tactical logistics services are uncommon in the country. The lack of a well -developed logistics industry in the country increases the need for retail chain companies to make investments in supply chain infrastructure. However, they are severely constrained by the unwillingness of commercial banks and financial institutions to lend for retailing, which is not an industry. External commercial borrowings are also barred even for the machinery and refrigeration equipment needed by the retail sector.

On contract farming also there has been progress in that several States have amended their laws to make contract farming possible. The success of contract farming for the food processing industry has been demonstrated in Punjab by Pespi

Foods Ltd. Organized retail can similarly benefit from contract farming and at the same time the farmers can gain if the retail companies invest in training the farmers, and in imparting skills in improved farming techniques as well as communication skills. However, for successful contract farming operations regulations are needed to ensure quick remedy against contract violations and speedy resolution of disputes. Many States have not framed the Rules under the Acts for dealing with these problems. A commonly voiced concern is also that the farmers should not lose their land and become bonded labourers.

4.5.2 Multiple License Requirements: The retail trade industry has represented that it has to secure a total of 45 licenses, clearances, registration certificates or notification requirements for each outlet and that its operational efficiency would increase considerably if a it had the facility of single window clearance.

4.5.3 Regulatory Requirements: These State laws have different provisions on opening and closing hours and on the working hours for women. All of them require the shops and offices to be closed for at least one day a week on a mandatory basis. Constraints on opening and closing hours limit the operations of retail outlets and inconvenience the clientele. Restrictive limitation on the working hours of women is anomalous when in the IT sector the limitations have been removed on the condition that transport would have to be provided by the employer to enable women to return home in the night. Compulsory closure of stores and offices for a day in the week is also not warranted because if worker's welfare is the aim it can be accomplished by requiring that employees should be given weekly off day on any fixed day by rotation.

In more ways than one the Shops & Establishment Act is outdated and the High Level Group recommends that the Government of India should set up a Committee consisting of representatives of Government, Trade Associations and the Unions to review the provisions and propose changes that take into account today's realities in terms of workplace practices, use of technology etc.

The practice at present is that the inspecting authorities hold the retailers also liable for any violations in compliance with the standards of Weights and Measures Act. The High Level Group found the argument of the retail industry compelling that as they purchase products from large numbers of suppliers, it is not practical for them to verify whether the manufacturers have complied with the provisions of the Act. The Act needs to be amended to make only the manufacturers and packers responsible for non-compliance and not the retailers.

The ESI was conceived of as a very good scheme for taking care of the healthcare problems of industrial employees. However, on account of poor implementation of the scheme a very small number of employees of shops and establishments are able to avail of its benefits. The experience of these employees is that issuance of ESI identity cards takes months, generally the doctors are not available, and medicines are in short supply. The requirement that ESI contribution be paid even in respect of temporary employees who, because of the short duration of their service, can never hope for any benefit from the ESI hospitals, is regarded as particularly onerous. The High Level Group suggests that the Government should set up a Committee to evaluate the performance of the ESI scheme and make suggestions for reform. Since now a number of health insurance companies have come up in the private sector employers/employees should be given the option of subscribing to alternative health insurance programmes.

The Essential Commodities Act, 1955 was enacted to ensure the easy availability of essential commodities to consumers and to protect them from exploitation by unscrupulous traders. Under the Act various State Governments had issued orders for licensing of dealers/retailers, regulation of stock limits, restricting the movement of food grains, compulsory purchase by the

Government under the system of levy and placing restrictions on the entertainment of guests. In 2001 a Committee comprising of Central Ministers and a number of Chief Ministers took the view that while the Essential Commodities Act could continue as an umbrella legislation a progressive dismantling of controls and restrictions was in the best interests of farmers, consumers and traders. Accordingly all restrictions including licensing requirement, stock limits and movement restrictions were dispensed with by the Central Government through the Removal of (Licensing requirements, Stock limits and Movement restrictions) on Specified Foodstuffs Order, 2002 under the Essential Commodities Act, 1955 on 15.2.2002. Dealers were allowed to freely buy, stock, sell, transport, sell, transport, distribute, dispose etc. any quantity in respect of wheat, paddy/rice, coarse grains, sugar, edible oilseeds and edible oils without requiring any license or permit therefore under any order issued under the Act.

In August 2006 the Central Government issued an order whereby controls were reintroduced temporarily for a period of six months in respect of wheat and pulses. This order has been extended periodically and is at present valid until 31st August 2008.

5

Healthcare Services

5.1 Introduction

Health security is one of the major components of human development. Good health is not only an end product of development but also a necessary condition for economic development. Improved health contributes to economic growth by reducing production losses due to illness of workers. There is a significant relation between income growth and health.

Health care is one of the functions of the State. According to the Directive Principles of State Policy laid down in the Constitution, raising the level of nutrition, and the standard of living and the improvement of public health are among the primary duties of the State. Improvement in the health status of the population has been one of the major thrust areas for the social development programmes of the country.

The World Health Assembly held in 1977 adopted a resolution which said that the main social target in the coming decades should be the attainment by every citizen of the world of a level of health that will permit him to lead a socially and economically productive life. The Assembly had set the year 2000 as the target date for achieving the objective. Subsequently, the Conference on Primary Health Care held at Alma Ata declared that primary health care is the key to attaining this target as part of development, and in the spirit of social justice. Since then, many countries have adopted primary health care as the strategy for social security. India has also adopted primary health care as the main instrument for achieving the goal of health for all. A vast network of institutions at primary, secondary and tertiary levels has been established for this purpose. The provision of primary health care services constitutes one of the seven Basic Minimum

Services included in the national agenda.

The primary health care infrastructure is intended to provide integrated promotive, curative and rehabilitative services to the population close to their residence. It is estimated that over 80 per cent of the health care needs of the population can be met by the primary health care infrastructure; only the rest may require referral to the secondary or tertiary health care institutions.

Nearly 30 per cent of India's population lives in urban areas. Due to the massive inflow of population to the towns and cities, the health status of urban slum dwellers is, at times, worse than that of the rural population. There has been a dearth of well planned and organized effort to provide primary health care services to the urban population within 2-3 kms of their residence and to link primary, secondary and tertiary care institutions in geographically defined areas. While an elaborate network of health services based on population norms has been established in the rural areas through group centres, primary health centres and community health centres, the services provided in these centres have, however, not been satisfactory.

The Planning Commission itself has admitted that the Primary Health Care System is facing the following problems.

- Persistent gaps in manpower and infrastructure especially at the primary health care level.
- Sub-optimal functioning of the infrastructure; poor referral services.
- Plethora of hospitals not having appropriate manpower, diagnostic and therapeutic services and drugs in government, voluntary and private sector.
- Massive inter-state and inter-district differences in performance, as assessed by health and demographic indices; availability and utilization of services are poorest in the most needy states/districts.
- Sub-optimal inter-sectoral coordination.
- Increasing dual disease burden of communicable and non-communicable diseases because of ongoing transitions in

demographic composition, lifestyle and environ-mental conditions.

- Technological advances which widen the spectrum of possible interventions.
- Increasing awareness and expectations of the population regarding health care services.
- Escalating costs of health care, ever widening gaps between what is possible and what the individual or the country can afford.

In spite of these deficiencies, primary health care is regarded as the most appropriate strategy for attaining the goal of health for all, within a reasonable time frame.

Health care is also an important component of social security. Indeed medical care is widely regarded as the primary branch of social security since health is of concern to all age groups and all categories of employees. All comprehensive social security programmes, therefore, make provision for medical care. The ILO Convention No. 130 and Recommendation No. 69 contain guidelines for the provision of medical care under social security.

In this connection the following question arises: when the State is committed to a policy of health for all, and has built up, or is building up a huge health infrastructure to achieve that objective, is it necessary or desirable to set up a parallel system of health care under social security? If not, what is the role of social security in the field of health care?

Social security and public health had historically developed independently. This had led to the existence of different operational practices and models, centres of interest and pressure groups. To overcome the obstacles that might be created by vested interests, a consensus should be achieved on two fundamental principles applicable to health policy; the principle of equity and that of efficiency.

The need for equity is based on the fact that health could not be considered exclusively as an individual phenomenon, but has to be treated as a social problem.

It should be obvious that if a separate system of health care were to be established for providing medical care to the unorganized sector which covers practically the whole population except for the small number of persons in the organized sector, it will be more or less parallel to the existing system of public medical service and will amount to complete duplication. There is hardly any justification for it. Considering, however, that the public medical service has not been satisfactory, it is equally obvious that there cannot be a total reliance on that system. It has to be supplemented by other measures. This is the rationale for a variety of health insurance schemes that have come up, or are coming up. The ESI Scheme, the CGHS and the Mediclaim policies of the GIC are the most well known among the health insurance schemes.

It is evident that there is need as well as scope for extension of health insurance both for raising additional finances necessary to increase access to medical services and for enhancing quality. The need is for optimal utilization of private and public resources and facilities. Although the 1983 National Health Policy reform encouraged health insurance services, there has been only a limited extension of such insurance through GIC-sponsored schemes since that time.

The available evidence is not clear on the health insurance priorities for workers in the unorganized sector. Most of them are more interested in ensuring the provision of primary, and some secondary health services, than to insure themselves against much less frequently occurring hospitalization costs.

If workers prefer to contribute to primary and some secondary health services, one could use the new concept of managing and financing of health care, particularly in rural areas. Under the Community Health Centres (CHC) scheme, the provision and financing of health care will be undertaken by communities characterized by strong social bonds and mutual trust. The CHC would provide preventive services, immunization, health promotion, family planning, maternal and childcare, and outpatient services to all its members, including drugs, for which a co-payment (part-payment) would be levied. Each community of about 1,000 people would have a health post serviced by one health worker paid by CHC, and a stock of generic drugs specified in the WHO essential drug list.

The CHC would also establish a primary health centre for a population of about 15,000 people, staffed by a doctor, a mid-wife, a clinical nurse, a primary care practitioner, a pharmacist, and an assistant. These centres would refer patients to the regional centres for tertiary care, possibly on the basis of a packaged foreign exchange or a capitation payment. Patients have the choice of obtaining free health services at the health posts and primary health centres or from private practitioners. When the service is obtained from a private practitioner, the CHC will only reimburse the patient 50% of its costs.

This new organization would mean a significant improvement over services currently provided by the government, which finances one sub-centre for a minimum of only 5,000 people and one primary health centre for 30,000 people. If the preference of workers is for insurance to counter the cost of hospitalization, then it may be advisable to follow the model developed by SEWA. It appears from their experience that the extension of worthwhile health coverage should be possible at affordable premium levels. In SEWA'S reckoning a satisfaction level of 50 per cent could be achieved towards reimbursement of a member's health expenses against a small annual premium of Rs. 15.

Thus, while basic health security has to be provided by the primary health care infrastructure, it may be supplemented by one or more of the various options indicated above. Considering the size and diversity of the population in India no one model would be adequate. It may be necessary to have a combination of schemes. As most of these schemes will be voluntary, development of such schemes may be left to the initiative of the people to form groups and to organize them according to their felt needs. Health insurance scheme of the ESI has an important role to play in supplementing the public medical service. It is, therefore, necessary to take all possible measures to improve its working and its expansion.

The expenditure on health comprises 5.2 percent of GDP with public health investment at 0.9 percent. Improvement in the health status of the population is a major thrust area under the social development programmes being undertaken in the country. This is sought to the achieved through improvement in the access to and utilization of health services in the country with special focus on under served and under privileged segments of the population. India has built up a vast health infrastructure and manpower at primary, secondary and tertiary care in government, voluntary and private sectors. Technological advances and improvement in access to health care technologies have resulted in a substantial improvement in health indices of the population and a steep decline in mortality. However, the extent of access to and utilization of health care has varied substantially between States, districts and different segments of society.

During the 1990s, the country has entered an era of dual disease burden. While communicable diseases have become more difficult to combat due to insecticide resistance among vectors, resistance to antibiotics in many bacteria and emergence of new diseases such as HIV increasing longevity and the changes in life style have resulted in the increasing prevalence of non-communicable diseases.

5.2 National Population Policy (2000)

The National Population Policy adopted in February 2000 affirms the commitment of the Government towards stabilizing the population of the country by providing for its citizens to make voluntary and informed decisions about their family size. The policy envisages certain National Socio-Demographic goals to be achieved by 2010 for paving the way for a stable population in the country by 2045, at a level consistent with the requirements of sustainable economic growth and social development. It also provides a policy for advancing goals and prioritizing strategies during the next decade, to meet the reproductive and child health needs of the people of India, and to achieve net replacement levels of fertility (Total Fertility Rate viz. TFR=2:1) by 2010.

It has been decided to relocate the National Population Stabilization Fund (NPSF) from the National Commission on Population to the Department of Family Welfare. The NPSF has been created with core funding of Rs. 100 crore from Government of India and will invite funds inter alia from the voluntary and corporate sector. NGOs etc. for strengthening the funding position for population stabilization programmes.

An Empowered Action Group (EAG) has been constituted in the Ministry of Health and Family Welfare with Union Minister for Health & Family Welfare as Chairman on 20th March 2001. The EAG aims at assisting states with weak socio demographic indicators to attain the goals listed in the National Population policy in the first instance the states of Bihar, Uttar Pradesh, Madhya Pradesh, Rajasthan, Orissa, Jharkhand, Uttaranchal and Chhattisgarh have been chosen for focussed attention.

Population Census 2001 results have shown a decline in the sex ratio in the age group 0-6 years in several States. For the country as a whole the child sex ratio is 927 girls per 1000 boys (Census 2001) which is much less than 945 recorded for the 1991 Census. The government is keen to strengthen the implementation mechanism of Pre-Natal Diagnostic Techniques (Regulation and Prevention of Misuse) Act, 1994 (PNDT Act).

The Mother NGO (MNGO) programme of the Department of Family Welfare has been recognized by the Planning Commission as a model scheme for adoption by other Ministries/Departments of the Government of India, for funding NGOs. The scheme has been revised extensively to make it more user-friendly, comprehensive and flexible.

While population stabilization is on the Concurrent List, health is a State subject. The reproductive and child health services reach community and household levels through the primary health care infrastructure inadequacies in the existing health infrastructure have led to gaps in coverage and outreach services in rural areas. The Pradhan Mantri Gramodaya Yojana (PMGY) for Primary Health Sector is an initiative to strengthen and revitalize the primary health infrastructure.

The Reproductive and Child Health Programme (RCH) was launched on 10th October 1997 and combines fertility regulation, safe motherhood, child survival and Reproductive Tract Infections (RT)/Sexually Transmitted Infections (STI). This programme is primarily implemented through the primary health care infrastructure. Independent surveys have shown that several states have achieved goals set for some aspect of the RCH programme during the Ninth Plan, demonstrating that these can be achieved within the existing infrastructure, manpower and inputs.

For improving obstetric care services, all C-category districts of the States of Uttar Pradesh, Bihar, Madhya Pradesh, Orissa, Haryana, Assam, and Nagaland are being supported to engage additional Auxiliary Nurse Midwives (ANMs) in 30 percent of the Sub-Centres. The scheme has been extended to six North Eastern states and Delhi. Similarly, states have been supported to engage contractual staff (Public Health Nurses and Lab. Technicians) to alleviate the problem of shortage of trained manpower in PHCs/CHCs and Sub-district hospitals.

A detailed programme has been initiated to provide RCH services in remote areas by holding RCH camps in those PHCs that are remote and remain unutilized. Initially during 2000-01, the scheme was implemented in 102 districts. It has since been extended to 76 more districts.

Vitamin A deficiency, which can lead to blindness, has been prevalent in the country, especially among the pre-school children. Under the programme for prevention of and control of vitamin A deficiency among children, five doses of vitamin

A are administered to all children under 3 years of age.

Iron deficiency (anemia) is widely prevalent not only in women of child-bearing age but also in young children. The National Family Health Survey-II (1998-99) revealed that 74.3 percent children under the age of 3 years were anemic. There is a marginal difference in the prevalence in the rural and urban areas. While 75.3 percent of rural children were found to be anemic, the prevalence in urban children was 70.8 percent. Under the National Programme iron folic acid tablets containing 20 mg of elemental iron and 0.1 mg of folic acid are provided at the sub-centre level.

The goal of the Universal Immunization Programme is to achieve 100 percent coverage of all eligible children and pregnant women. To strengthen the outreach services in 151 weaker districts of 28 States, a scheme of RCH Outreach Services has been implemented where inputs have been provided to increase coverage and improve quality of immunization.

It is estimated that prior to the Pulse Polio Immunization Programme around 2.5 lakh children used to get afflicted by polio each year. The reported number of cases in 1987 was 28,257 which was estimated to be around 8 to 10 per cent of the actual cases. In order to establish a better surveillance system, National Polio Surveillance Project (NPSP) was launched in October 1997 under which a network of 8000 reporting units have been established which is being supervised by over 220 Surveillance Medical Officers. The NPSP has been able to sustain an international standard surveillance system for polio since then. The number of reported polio cases declined considerably from 28,257 reported in 1987 to 268 in 2001. However, during 2002, 1211 polio cases have been reported till 3rd December, 2002 of which 990 cases are from Uttar Pradesh, and 81 from Bihar.

The Information, Education and Communication (IEC) component of the National Family Welfare Programme aims to generate demand for the range of Family Welfare and

Reproductive and Child Health Services available, with the help of the States Districts and NGOs. A new National Communication strategy has been put in place in tune with the National Population Policy 2000, to chalk out a systematic campaign in which the district is the focal point. A crucial feature of the new strategy is the recognition that increasingly, IEC work will have to be decentralized to the States, Districts and community levels.

The agenda for population stabilization is multi-sectoral which necessitates decentralization and convergence across sectors. In cooperation with State Governments, the Department of Family Welfare, is bringing about a convergence between the NGOs, the Self Help Groups (run by the Department of Rural Development) the Zila Saksharta Samitis (run by the Department of Education), the social marketing organizations (overseen by Department of Family Welfare) and the panchayati raj institutions, to improve integrated service delivery at community and household levels. Survivors' benefits are provided under the National Family Benefit Scheme and other schemes like the Janshree Bima Yojna. We recommend that the National Family Benefit Scheme should be linked to the National Pension Scheme (suggested above) and the Janshree Bima Yojna, rationalizing the quantum of benefits.

Every person below the poverty line, whether employed or not, may be paid an allowance for the maintenance of children and to enable them to send children to school and not to work.

5.3 Nutrition Support

Although the country has been able to eliminate nutritional deficiency syndrome like pellagra, beriberi, scurvy etc., yet chronic energy deficiency among adults, under-nutrition among children and micronutrient deficiencies are still prevalent across all section of the population. The country has adopted a multi-sectoral and multi-pronged strategy to combat these problems and to improve the nutritional status of the population.

One half of the children under the age of five years in India are moderately or severely malnourished, 30 per cent of newborn children are significantly under weight and nearly 60 percent of women are anemic. Under the Integrated Child Development Scheme (ICDS) the Department of Women and Child Development implements the food supplementation programme for improving nutritional status of mothers and children. Ministry of Health and Family Welfare implements programmes for tackling major micronutrient deficiencies such as Vitamin A and Iodine deficiency etc.

To address the needs of undernourished infants and children below 3 years, 15 per cent of the total Additional Central Assistance (ACA) is earmarked for the nutrition component under the Pradhan Mantri Gramodaya Yojana (PMGY). ACA under the nutrition component of PMGY is an additionality for providing nutrition to children in 0-3 years. States are required to ensure that all below poverty line (BPL) children [as also unreached and marginalized] in 0-3 years are registered for PMGY and the provided requisite nutrition for meeting the gap in the Recommended Dietary Allowance [in contrast with providing only normative supplementary nutrition] by supplementing the States' commitment for supplementary nutrition with adequate ACA under PMGY. During 2000-01 and 2001-02 the Department of Women and Child Development was the nodal Department for the implementation of the nutrition component of the programme. From 1st April 2002, the Planning Commission is directly implementing the scheme.

Nutrition Support is one of the Basic Minimum Services included in the National Agenda. There are two major programmes which provide food supplements to the vulnerable segments of the population; these are the Supplementary Nutrition programme and the midday Meal programme.

Special Nutrition programme is one of the important components of the Integrated Child Development Services programmes. The target group receiving found supplementation is children between the age of 6 months and 6 years and pregnant and lactating mothers. The beneficiaries receive supplements through the ICDS infrastructure, which is funded by the Department of Women and Child Development.

The programme of Nutritional Support to Primary Education, popularly known as Midday Meal Scheme, was launched in 1995 as a fully funded Centrally Sponsored Scheme. Under this scheme, all school children in the primary schools in government and government-aided schools are to be covered. Ideally, a hot meal is provided to the children at school for 10 months in the year. The foodgrains are delivered directly at the district level by the Food Corporation of India, under instructions from the Department of Education in the Government of India. So far, the Scheme has not been universalized, but once it is, the annual expenditure would be of the order of Rs. 2,226 crore going up each year on account of the increase in cost. There are some complaints about the working of the Midday Meal Scheme. It has been suggested that these complaints be looked into and the programme made more effective and meaningful.

5.4 National Nutrition Mission

The Prime Minister, in his Independence Day speech on 15th August, 2001 announced the setting up of a National Nutrition Mission. Under this Mission, subsidized foodgrains would be made available to adolescent girls and expectant and nursing mothers, belonging to below-poverty-line families.

A two tier structure is envisaged for the Mission. The National Nutrition Mission would be headed by the Prime Minister and its Executive Committee would be under the Human Resource Development Minister. Composition and Terms of Reference of the Mission are under finalization and decision in this regard is expected soon.

A National Nutrition Mission will soon be launched in selected nutrionally backward districts of the country to further carry forward the goals of National Nutrition Policy.

5.5 Public Health System

Public institutions played a dominant role in the Indian Healthcare sector in the past, in the urban as well as in the rural areas. However, the public healthcare has been on a serious decline during the last two or three decades because of non-availability of medical and paramedical staff, diagnostic services and medicines. Equally distressing is the fact that essential therapeutic drugs are not supplied in most public health institutions with the exception of some States. Consequently there has been a pronounced decline in the percentage of cases of hospitalized treatment in Government hospitals and a corresponding increase in the percentage treated in private hospitals. Despite higher costs in the private sector, this shift shows the people's growing lack of trust in the public system. Critical shortage of health personnel, inadequate incentives, poor working conditions, lack of transparency in posting of doctors in rural areas, absenteeism, long wait, inconvenient clinic hours, poor outreach, time of service, insensitivity to local needs, inadequate planning, management, and monitoring of service/facilities appear to be the main reasons for low utilization.

5.6 Medical Value Travel in India

What is significant is that the hospitals established by the private corporate players are of world class. They have not only the latest medical technological facilities but also the services of Indian doctors and nurses with a high degree of proficiency. Corporate hospitals are completely equipped, up market and proficient and can measure up, or even outshine, any hospital in the west. India's value proposition is it being able to offer highly cost competitive medical treatment with the most up-to-date technological advances. The quality of their service coupled with the highly competitiveness charged by them for common surgeries has made India an attractive destination for medical value travel.

The Indian Government has moved to provide visa facilities for the medical tourists. The main clientele comes from the SAARC countries but an increasing number of NRIs settled in the US and the UK have also been availing of the healthcare services in India. There is a good prospect of patients coming from the Middle East in future. The main impediment for medical tourists coming from the UK and US for major surgeries is the fact that the insurance companies are generally not willing to cover treatment in India. However, the cost savings involved in getting treatment done in India is bound to result in the insurance company imposed barriers breaking down in future. Already some hospitals are entering into alliance with international insurance companies for making it possible to send patients to India for treatment.

The competitiveness of India in medical value travel is enhanced by the attractiveness of the alternative systems of medicine, Ayurveda in particular, for the foreign tourists. A large number of tourists, both domestic and foreign, undergo treatment under Ayurveda not only for improving their fitness and well-being but also for curing many types of chronic diseases. For the regulation of Ayurveda clinics and for ensuring that they employ techniques in accordance with traditional methods the Ministry of Health has issued guidelines to be used by the States. Accordingly Kerala, the most popular destination for tourists for treatment under Ayurveda has promulgated an Ordinance regulating Ayurveda Health Centres.

The Ordinance requires registration of such centres and prescribes the facilities and medical staff that they must have in order to run them. The unique position that Kerala enjoys with respect to Ayurveda is due to the fact that the treatment in the State has proved effective in dealing with certain diseases, which are incurable by other systems. The State is also well endowed with herbs and medicinal plants, which are used for treatment.

5.7 Indian Medical Professionals Abroad

One of the main reasons for the international competitiveness of private healthcare institutions in India is the quality of Indian medical professionals. While the quality is highly variable across the country the best professionals in India match the quality of professionals in the developed countries. For several decades Indian medical professionals have been serving not only in the Middle East but also in several English speaking developed countries including the USA and the UK.

India ranks at the top of nations whose physicians are working in the major developed countries and holds the second position to Philippines in respect of nurses.

India has also emerged as a supplier of other categories of healthcare professionals to a number of countries, particularly radiologists, laboratory technicians, dental hygienists, physiotherapists and medical rehabilitation workers.

India's strong position as a supplier of healthcare professionals is notwithstanding the fact that the medical qualifications awarded by Indian institutions are not recognized by the authorities in the developed countries and the professionals have to qualify in examinations held by those authorities. As a measure of reciprocity Indian Medical Council also does not recognize the qualifications awarded by those authorities.

5.8 Health Insurance

Traditionally healthcare insurance in the country has been limited to the Employees State Insurance Schemes (ESIS) for industrial workers, the Central Government Health Scheme (ECHS) for employees and pensioners of the Central Government and the Ex Servicemen Contributory Health Scheme (ECSH) for the former Armed Forces Personnel. After general insurance was opened up to the private sector and further to FDI, there has been a considerable expansion of health insurance, covering mainly the urban upper-middle class. However, healthcare insurance schemes have experienced problems such as high premium, delay in settling claims and non-transparent procedures in deciding reimbursements. The system of Third Party Administrators (TPAs) has facilitated cash payments and expanded access to providers and as a result delivery of healthcare services to the upper middle class has improved. Other segments of the population, the BPL categories in particular, have remained deprived of the benefits of health insurance in the country.

Side by side with the development of health insurance on a commercial basis the country has seen the emergence of Community Based Health Insurance (CBHI). CBHI is a not-for- profit insurance scheme managed by the members themselves on the basis of collective pooling of health risks. CBHI schemes are being operated by organizations such as ACCORD, BAIF, Karuna Trust, SEWA, DHAN Foundation and VHS.

5.9 Challenges Facing Healthcare Sector in India

The competitiveness of healthcare services in the country suffers from under-regulation on the whole but over-regulation on the medical education front. Medical professionals are regulated through Central legislation, viz., the Indian Medical Councils Act, the Dentist Act and the Nursing Council Act. These laws provide for the setting up of regulatory councils at the National and State levels. The National Councils prescribe norms and standards of education, while the State Councils deal primarily with registration and enforcement of these standards. The Ministry of Health &Family Welfare has developed Indian Public Health Standards (IPHS) for certain Governmental clinical establishments viz., Community Health Centres (CHC), Primary Health Centres (PHC) and Sub-Centres, which are implemented through administrative means.

Standards are also being evolved for the larger hospitals, up to 500 beds. A few States and Union Territories have enacted laws (The Bombay Nursing Homes Act, 1949; Delhi Nursing Homes Act, 1953; and Tamil Nadu Private Clinical

Establishments Act, 1997) for registration and regulation of nursing and clinical establishments, but they were not comprehensive in that they did not cover laboratories and diagnostic centres, and there were deficiencies in laying down minimum standards. More importantly their implementation has remained ineffective. There has been resistance from some stakeholders against the introduction of law for the regulation of health care service providers because of the fear of Inspector Raj. Opposition to regulation of health service providers has also been fuelled by the exemption provided in some of the State laws for the public health institutions. On the other hand there is skepticism among policy makers whether publicly funded healthcare institutions will be able to adhere to the standards. The multiplicity in the types of clinical establishments has also daunted policy makers from undertaking the task of formulating minimum standards, which are a prerequisite for effective regulation.

At the Central level, some specific aspects of healthcare services have been regulated through legislation, such as management of medical waste, setting up of blood banks, and pre-natal diagnostic tests, but there is absence of an overall statutory framework for the licensing of healthcare establishments such as hospitals, nursing homes and clinics, and laying down the minimum standards that must be met.

There are rules for the registration of medical practitioners and separate regulations for professional conduct, etiquette and ethics. The latter contain certain recommendatory rules, such as use of generic names of drugs, but also mandatory rules, such as for the maintenance of medical records of indoor patients for minimum period of three years and maintenance of a register of certificates issued. There is however a serious regulatory gap in the country in that there are no mandatory standards prescribed and enforced for hospitals, nursing homes, clinics, as well as establishments undertaking diagnosis or treatment of disease. The standards for hospitals, for instance, should cover all aspects ranging from building and fire safety to availability of potable water and from basic laboratory services to employment of health professionals. According to international best practice license is granted initially on the basis of some form of external evaluation of compliance with the prescribed minimum standards.

The commencement in 2006 of an accreditation programme for secondary and tertiary hospitals by the National Accreditation Board for Hospitals & Healthcare Providers (NABH), a constituent board of the Quality Council of India, represents a strong attempt to improve the quality of healthcare establishments in the country. Accreditation is a voluntary process, involving evaluation of an organization's compliance with pre-established performance standards. The organization is granted accreditation if it is assessed to meet an acceptable level compliance, or it may be given a conditional accreditation.

NABH has so far granted accreditation to 11 hospitals and 43 are in various stages of evaluation. It has 120 qualified assessors on its panel, comprising senior clinicians, hospital administrators and nursing supervisors, who are assigned the task of carrying out the evaluation.

An accreditation system such as what has been established in India is the best way of improving the quality of performance of clinical establishments. The challenge in the country is for more and more clinical establishments to take advantage of the accreditation system in order to improve the quality of healthcare service in the country. As for clinical establishment run by the Central and State Governments the first step should be that they adhere to the minimum standards prescribed under the proposed legislation, but as a subsequent step they should also come forward and take advantage of the accreditation system.

Medical education is highly regulated and there is an access barrier for setting up new medical and dentist colleges. Eligibility for setting up medical or dentist colleges is limited to the following organizations:

- A State Government/ Union territory;
- A University;
- An autonomous body promoted by Central and State Government;
- A Society registered under the Societies Registration Act, 1860(21 of 1860) or corresponding Acts in States; or
- A public religious or charitable trust registered under the Trust Act, 1882 (2 of 1882) or the Wakf Act, 1954 (29 of 1954).

What is significant here is that the corporate sector is not eligible and only not-for-profit organizations can apply. The private sector medical and dental colleges that have been established in large numbers have all done so by setting up not-for-profit societies.

For medical colleges another access barrier is the condition that the applicant must own or possess a suitable single plot of land measuring not less than 25 acres by way of 99 years lease for the construction of the college. For dental colleges the requirement is less restrictive and only an area of 5 acres is required and that too for a minimum period of 30 years. For nursing colleges it is significant that companies are eligible to set up nursing colleges and schools and there is no bar on commercial (for-profit) organizations. Further instead of the requirement for a specific area of available land, the requirement is for built up space. However, here too there is an access barrier as the requirement of a large size campus of more than 23 000 square feet for the college and 30,000 for the hostel is out of proportion of the requirement for a 50-seat college.

For the paramedical personnel there several institutions, in the States but also in the private sector but these are unregulated and there is lack of uniformity in the training imparted. For regulating training of paramedics it is proposed to set up the Paramedics Council and a Bill for the same has already been introduced in Parliament. Separately, there is also a proposal in the Ministry of Health & Family Welfare to set up a National Institute of Paramedical Sciences (with branches in New Delhi and Chennai) for undertaking and coordinating training programmes in the country in collaboration with State Governments. The Ministry is proposing to use distance education to ensure large coverage of the training programmes.

Besides the problem of the numbers of healthcare personnel there is an acute problem of quality as well. Some of the private colleges are produce graduates far below the standards required but the Government colleges have also deteriorated, in part because of shortage of staff, the vacancies remaining unfilled because of unattractive remuneration. In Government medical colleges another reason for deterioration of the quality of medical graduates is that they do not get the opportunity to observe the treatment of patients because of the fall in the number of patients coming to Government hospitals for treatment.

While the middle class has benefited from the entry of the private health insurance companies the real challenge is to enhance access to healthcare for the poorer sections of the population through health insurance. The healthcare insurance companies in the public or in the private sector cannot take up this challenge because the poorer sections (30 crore of BPL population) does not have the capacity to pay the premium at rates required to run the programme on a commercial basis. A health insurance programme, which covers the BPL categories, will also give the choice to the population in these categories to turn to the healthcare providers in the private sector. In order to make the implementation of such a programme feasible it would be necessary to introduce a smart card system for the beneficiaries. Such a scheme will not only benefit the poorer sections but also private healthcare service providers, whose business will expand.

6

Insurance Services

Until recently, insurance services in India were provided by the public sector i.e. life insurance by the Life Insurance Corporation of India (LIC) since the mid-1950s, and general insurance by the General Insurance Corporation (GIC) and its four subsidiaries since the 1970s. The insurance industry was opened up to the private sector in August 2000. The primary objective of liberalisation in the insurance sector was to deepen insurance penetration by enlarging consumer choices through product innovation. The increased competition has led to rapid product innovations for catering to the diverse requirements of the various segments of the population. Besides statutory commitments in respect of weaker sections of society, competitive pressures are pushing life insurers to adopt innovative marketing strategies to extend insurance penetration, especially targeting lower income groups. Insurance industry in India is broadly classified into (a) life insurance and (b) non-life insurance business.

6.1 Insurance Industry Prior to Reforms of Late 1990s

People in general have all along been grumbling against LIC's monopolistic exploitation, poor service and high premium rates. Same was the case with general insurance business which was also monopolised by the Government. Articulating the inefficiency of the Government-controlled insurance sector and the need to allow private participation in it, the Ninth Five Year Plan (1997-2002) observed, "...the average premium charged by the insurance companies in India tends to be relatively high due to obsolete and rigid actuarial practices and inefficient operations. There is a pressing need to reorient the insurance sector in India in a manner that it fulfils its principal mandate of providing risk cover. It is unlikely that this sector would attain the requisite degree of efficiency and professionalism unless it is exposed to a certain degree of competition." [1]

Being a monopoly of the Government, the insurance industry in India could not develop on modern and competitive lines after Independence. It suffered from various infirmities. There can be several parameters to measure the productivity in the insurance sector. These can be in terms of collection of premium per development officer, issuance of documents per employee, claim settlement per employee, underwriting results, yield on investment income etc. Productivity of the Indian insurance industry in terms of these indicators was quite low prior to the reforms of late 1990s.

The adoption of information technology in the industry was not to the desired extent. There was lack of computerisation and hence database for being utilised by the insurance companies, agents and consumers. Technology infrastructure, such as electronic fund transfer, internet, automatic teller machines, interactive voice response, electronic data inter change, was almost non-existent. The use of internet and e-commerce for selling the insurance products had not yet commenced in the industry.

Insurance policies in the segments of health and household risks were not properly marketed and publicised. The entire thrust on health insurance was on products after the occurrence of illness while the preventive aspects were ignored. The products covering environmental and financial risks were non-existent. Another area, which remained untapped, was the development of saving-linked non-life insurance policies.

By and large, the quality of insurance services provided was low. The quality of insurance services is evaluated, inter alia, in terms of expeditious settlement of claims, delivery of policy documents and after sales services. The delivery of insurance documents took long times. There was neither proper control on management expenses nor optimal utilisation of investible resources.

6.2 R.N. Malhotra Committee on Insurance Reforms, 1994

In an effort to change India from being a controlled economy to a market-driven one, inviting participation of private investors, both foreign and Indian, the Government of India initiated a programme of economic reforms in 1991. India, being a member of World Trade Organisation (WTO), is also committed to integrate the Indian economy with that of the other member nations in a phased manner.

In this background, the Government set up in April 1993, a high-powered committee headed by R.N. Malhotra, former Governor, Reserve Bank of India to examine the structure of the insurance industry and recommend changes to make it more efficient and competitive, keeping in view the structural changes in other parts of the financial system of the economy. The Committee interacted with the insurance companies, their staff unions, various chambers of commerce, trade bodies and a cross section of the country's public and analysed the present Indian insurance industry. The Committee, which submitted its report on January 7, 1994, felt that the insurance regulatory apparatus should be activated even in the nationalised insurance sector, and recommended, inter alia, the establishment of a strong and effective Insurance Regulatory Authority (IRA), in the form of a statutory autonomous board on the lines of Securities and Exchange Board of India (SEBI). The Committee observed (a) Indian insurance industry lacks depth, diversity and reach, both geographically as well as in terms of insurable population, as there was immensely vast potential yet to be tapped, (b) it provides poor customer service in terms of pricing, adequacy and appropriateness of covers and the much needed and timely claims settlement and (c) it lacks the global dimensions having remained in isolation too long.

The year 1999 will go down in the insurance history of

India as a landmark year when, after prolonged hesitation, Government of India pushed through the Insurance Bill opening up the insurance sector to private players, almost 6 years after the submission of the Report of the Committee.

The public sector monopoly of insurance business was ended with the enactment of the Insurance Regulatory and Development Act, 1999. The insurance business was thrown open for private participation (including foreign equity participation up to 26 per cent of the paid-up capital). Further, the Insurance Regulatory and Development Authority (IRDA) Act, was enacted in 1999 and a separate Insurance Regulatory and Development Authority was set up. In order to ensure solvency of insurers and protection of policyholders' interests, the IRDA Act stipulates prudential norms for investments and service obligations in the less-lucrative rural sector. Following this, the Insurance Regulatory and Development Authority (IRDA) was set up on April 19, 2000. Its major functions include (a) regulation of investment funds by insurance companies, (b) adjudication of disputes between insurers and intermediaries and (c) supervision of Tariff Advisory Committee. The IRDA has been notifying regulations, from time to time, which, inter alia, pertain to registration of Indian insurance companies, insurance advertisements and disclosures, licensing of insurance agents and intermediaries, reinsurance, and obligation of insurers to rural and social sectors.

The insurance industry was opened up to the private sector in August 2000. The primary objective of liberalization in the insurance sector was to deepen insurance penetration by enlarging consumer choices through product innovation. The increased competition in the insurance sector has led to product innovations for catering to the diverse requirements of various segments of the population.

Commercial banks and non-banking financial companies satisfying the prescribed criteria have also been permitted to enter the insurance business with prior approval of the Reserve

Bank of India.

The avowed objective of IRDA Act is to provide for an authority to protect the interests of policyholders, to regulate, to promote and to ensure orderly growth of the insurance business in India.

The opening of the life insurance industry has benefited consumers in a number of ways: There has been an explosion in the choice of products, service levels have improved and price wars have brought down term insurance rates and administration charges in unit-linked policies.

Indian insurance industry remained a state-owned monopoly for more than 40 years in the case of life and not less than 25 years in the case of non-life. It remained in a cloistered world of its own The reasons then prevailing which prompted the state ownership are no longer valid in view of the rapidly changing global as well as local milieu.

6.3 Regulations and Controls

The supervisory control of insurance companies is exercised by Insurance Regulatory and Development Authority (IRDA) and these powers flow from Insurance Act, 1938 as well as from IRDA Act, 1999. IRDA Act 1999 states: "Subject to the provisions of this Act and any other law for the time being in force, the Authority shall have the duty to regulate, promote and ensure orderly growth of insurance business and reinsurance business."

Regulatory and supervisory powers of the IRDA are wide and pervasive. These can be summarised as under.

- Registration/Licensing: Any company proposing to enter in the insurance business has to apply to the authority for registration certificate. The authority has the powers to issue the licence subject to its satisfaction that the proposed company is financially sound and has the managerial expertise to run the business. The authority has also got the powers to renew it, modify it or even suspend and cancel such registration.

- Product and its Pricing: The authority shall be satisfied about the nature of the product and its pricing before it is placed for marketing amongst the consumers. The powers to control the price of the product is in addition to the premium rates which are fixed by the Tariff Advisory Committee (TAC) constituted under section 64U of Insurance Act, 1938. Chairman of the authority is also ex-officio Chairman of TAC. The authority should also be satisfied with the terms and conditions mentioned in the policy documents.
- Investment of Funds: The investment policy of the insurance companies is governed by the broad guidelines framed by the authority. It may direct the insurer to invest certain proportion of their funds in specified securities. For instance, the present directives are that general insurance companies have to invest minimum of 30 per cent of their funds in government securities and 15 per cent in housing projects including purchase of fire fighting equipments by state governments. Only 55 per cent of the funds may be invested in market securities and amongst market securities only in approved securities.
- Solvency Margin: The authority has to ensure that insurers maintain the solvency margin as laid down in the Act. In case companies fail to comply with solvency margin requirements, the authority can initiate disciplinary action against the defaulting companies.
- Appointment of Actuary: As per the directives of the authority, it is mandatory for insurer to appoint an actuary. The qualifications of actuary have been laid down. The functions and duties of actuary have been prescribed by the authority.
- Appointment to Chief Executive/Managing Director: It is obligatory on the part of insurance companies to take prior approval of the authority before appointing chief executive, managing director or whole time director in the company. The authority has also been vested with the

power to remove any managerial person and also appoint any additional director in the company, if so desired.

- Power of Investigation and Inspection: The authority can institute any inquiry against the insurer to investigate the affairs of the company and for this purpose can appoint any person as investigator. Based on the report, authority can take disciplinary action against the insurer including suspension of its registration.
- Accounts and Balance Sheets: The insurers are required to prepare a balance sheet, a profit and loss account, a separate account of receipts and payments and a revenue account in respect of each class of business. These are to be audited by a qualified auditor.
- Intermediaries: The authority shall also monitor the activities of intermediaries who are being engaged by the insurers to market their products. The licence to the agents will be issued by the authority. As and when brokers are allowed to operate, they will also have to obtain the licence from the authority.
- Surveyors and Loss Assessors: The qualifications for surveyors to be eligible to obtain a licence are prescribed by the authority. Their licences are also being issued by the authority.
- Reinsurance: Reinsurance programmes of insurance companies are being monitored by the authority on a continuous basis. As per the directives of the authority, insurance companies are required to cede a part of their premium income to designated Indian reinsurer. Insurers are supposed to keep authority apprised about their insurance programme, both outward and inward, and seek authority's approval.

6.4 Post-liberalisation Developments in Insurance Business

The Indian insurance industry has witnessed a sea-change since opening up to private players in 1999. The liberalisation has transformed the industry's outlook towards the vast Indian market. The spurt in the number of players has led to innovation in product development and distribution channels, thus treating the Indian customer to a whole new range of insurance products – each suited to match unique requirements of different societal segments.

The driving force behind the record growth of the industry is the increasing demand for specialised covers by customers. The customer profile is also changing with the introduction of a large number of private participants, divergent intermediaries such as agents, brokers, corporate agents, and bancassurance partners. With increasing buying capacity, asset procurement has been on the rise. This is turn has set the trend for increasing demand to protect assets against eventualities, including natural calamities.

Competition has become an essential ingredient in this scenario with guaranteed benefits to the customer and the society at large. It is evident that the customer has a wider menu to choose from and customer service benchmarks have begun to improve as a result of competitive pressures. Even for companies, it is beneficial to have others sharing the responsibility of increasing awareness, initiating policy changes and forcing insurers to recognise customers' needs, exploiting new opportunities, taking some risks in venturing into newer market areas and investing in people.

The ultimate objective of reforms is to increase insurance-density and insurance penetration levels by designing more tailor-made products for customers, both individuals and institutions.

The concept of bancassurance has also caught up. Almost all banks are marketing one or the other insurance policy. The fact that some have an insurance joint venture simply aids the process. The selling of insurance products by banks gives a seal of credibility in the minds of the individual. Bancassurance has emerged as a key distribution channel for both life and non-life insurance.

Agents and brokers will increasingly become an important part of the Indian insurance scene. With agents working on behalf of insurers and brokers on behalf of the insured, they both will enable the client receive the best advice on the most suitable insurance products. Also they allow the insurer reach parts of the country where the companies—geographically and otherwise—may find it impractical to expand their corporate presence.

Third-party administrators (TPA) have helped in the popularisation and spread of health insurance through customisation of products and promotion of cashless hospitalisation. Modifications in the mode of payment of insurance premium by allowing credit cards have facilitated easier distribution of insurance through the Internet and also via telemarketing.

Insurance along with biotechnology, business process outsourcing (BPO) and software has provided tremendous job opportunities. Following these prospects, the number of training schools is on the rise and management institutes are increasingly including courses on insurance in their curriculum.

6.5 New Initiatives

Numerous new initiatives have been taken by the private players, and even by the LIC. Some insurers such as ICICI Pru-Life have fulfilled their mission to be a scale player in the mass market by introducing a complete range of products to meet the individual needs of customers. Others have taken a more focused approach, introducing select products that they believe hold potential and fill market gaps. Service standards are being set and implemented and a series of distribution channels have thrown open new opportunities.

With heightened awareness and consumer education there are more customer-friendly products and a willingness to view life insurance as an integral part of one's financial portfolio. Insurance is no longer a poorly-understood product pushed onto the people or a product only to be bought hurriedly at the time of the closing of the financial year to avail tax benefits.

New private players have pioneered many significant trends as, for example, the introduction of products which do not have long-term guarantees. In an environment where interest rates are volatile, the days of long-term, high-guaranteed return products are over. Products are now priced flexibly, realistically and sustainably. With greater education, consumers are in a better position to understand the risks and the benefits.

The introduction of unit-linked products has brought about a new level of transparency and flexibility to what was always considered a black box product. Policyholders now have the choice of deciding how much premium they want to pay, the level of their sum assured and fund in which they would like to invest their money. Charges are disclosed upfront, and NAVs and portfolio allocations of the various funds are available on a regular basis. Though such products are more complex than their traditional counterparts, the opportunities they offer to the policyholder make them appealing to a wider range of investors.

Apart from protection, life insurers are being recognised for their ability to manage long-term retirement savings and pension funds. In fact, insurers such as ICICI Prudential were among the first to recognise the need for structured retirement planning among the Indian populace and to invest the necessary resources to build this segment.

Not only has there been a change in the structure and nature of products and the segments they address, but also in the way they are sold. From being a purely advisor-driven business, the insurance sector has seen the emergence of a number of channels, including bancassurance, corporate agents and direct marketing.

Almost all leading banks have tied up with insurance companies, both general and life, to distribute their products to accountholders. It is a win-win deal for all the parties involved.

The customer gets yet another product from an institution he already trusts, the bank has the opportunity to expand its product offerings and receive fee-income, and the insurer gets the benefits of a larger footprint, without the related investment. Judging from the progress made thus far, it seems that bancassurance is here to stay.

Another area of vast improvement is in service attitude and delivery. From a system that left policyholders running from pillar-to-post to get claims, service levels are steadily rising to make the customer the focus of every initiative. In fact, customers need not rely solely on their advisor, but have the option to reach the life insurer directly. For customers, there are multiple touch points—contact centres, e-mail, facsimile, websites—which enable the customer to get in touch with insurance companies quickly, easily and directly.

In some companies, advisors too have been given access to information that they need to have. They can get onto the insurer's website or they can access computers from the insurer's offices and download information on their customers, read industry news and view their commission statements. In all cases, the advisor or customer is in control of the process – response time has come down dramatically and information availability has become immediate.

As with privatisation in any industry, the benefits are not restricted to the customer, but extend to the society at large, by generating employment opportunities for thousands.

6.6 Broad-based Insurance Sector

In developing countries, one important character of insurance business and of long-term life insurance, in particular, is that insurance policies are generally a combination of risk coverage and savings. The savings component in the insurance policies is seen as a possible source of competition for the banking industry, as the insurance industry develops on a competitive basis. There are, however, other considerations that point to the possible complementarities and synergies between the insurance and banking business.

The most important source of complementarity arises due to the critical role that banks play in distributing and marketing of insurance products. So far, direct branch network of LIC and GIC and their subsidiaries together with their agents have been instrumental in marketing of insurance products in India. With further simplification of insurance products, the vast branch network and the depositor base of commercial banks are expected to play an important role in marketing insurance products over the counter. The eagerness on the part of several banks to enter into insurance business following the opening up of the industry to private participation reflects this emerging process.

In line with the regulations on registration of Indian insurance companies as issued by the Insurance Regulatory and Development Authority (IRDA) and subsequent Government Notification specifying 'insurance' as a permissible form of business that could be undertaken by banks under Section 6(1)(o) of the Banking Regulation Act, 1949, commercial banks were permitted in August 2000 to set up insurance joint ventures on a risk participation basis and also to undertake insurance business as agents of insurance companies on a fee basis, without any risk participation by banks and their subsidiaries.

The RBI, in recognition of the symbolic relationship between banking and the insurance industries, has identified three routes for banks' participation in the insurance business.

- Providing fee-based insurance services without risk participation.
- Investing in an insurance company for providing infrastructure and services support.
- Setting up of a separate joint venture insurance company with risk participation.

The third route, due to its risk aspects, involves compliance to stringent entry norms. Further, the bank has to maintain an arms length relationship between its banking business and its insurance outfit. For banks entering into insurance business with risk participation, the prescribed entity also enables to avoid possible regulatory overlaps between the Reserve Bank and the Government/ IRDA. The joint venture insurance company would be subjected entirely to the IRDA/government regulations.

With effect from October 2002, commercial banks were allowed to undertake referral business through their network of branches with the prior approval of the IRDA and the RBI. The requirement of such approval from the RBI was dispensed with in September 2003.

Non-banking Financial Companies (NBFCs) in Insurance Business: In June 2000, NBFCs registered with the RBI were permitted, with prior approval of the Reserve Bank, to set up insurance joint ventures for undertaking insurance business with risk participation and also to undertake insurance business as agents of insurance companies on a fee basis, without any risk participation subject to satisfaction of some eligibility criteria. This facility was later extended to financial institutions in November 2001.

In February 2004, it was decided to allow NBFCs registered with the RBI to take up insurance agency business on a fee basis and without risk participation, without the approval of the Reserve Bank subject to certain conditions.

Besides commercial banks, rural community-operative credit institutions are also envisaged as an important vehicle for distributing insurance products in under-served rural areas. The Task Force to Study the Community-operative Credit System and Suggest Measures for its Strengthening (Chairman: J. Capoor) noted that this could have an attendant benefit of portfolio diversification for these institutions.

In August 2003, a decision was taken to allow financially strong scheduled primary (urban) co-operative banks having a minimum net worth of Rs.100 crore and complying with certain other norms to undertake insurance business as corporate agents without risk participation.

In October 2004, regional rural banks (RRBs) were allowed to undertake, with prior permission of the RBI, insurance business as corporate agents without risk participation, subject to fulfilling certain terms and conditions such as positive net worth, compliance with prudential norms, NPAs not exceeding 10 per cent, continuous profits in the last 3 years and no accumulated losses. Besides, subject to certain conditions, they have also been allowed to undertake insurance business on a referral basis, without any risk participation, through their network of branches.

6.7 FDI in the Insurance Sector

FDI in the insurance sector up to 26 per cent (raised to 49 per cent in the 2004-05 budget) is allowed under the automatic route subject to licence from the Insurance Regulatory and Development Authority. In addition to automatic approval for new companies, such approval can also be granted for existing companies proposing to induct foreign equity, and for existing companies with an expansion programme. The additional requirements are the following.

- The increase in equity level must result from the expansion of the equity base of the existing company.
- The money to be remitted should be in foreign currency.
- The proposed expansion programme should be predominantly in the sector(s) under automatic route.

For existing companies without an expansion programme, the additional requirements for eligibility for automatic approval are the following.

1. They should be engaged predominantly in industries under the automatic route.
2. The increase in equity level must be from expansion of the equity base.
3. The foreign equity must come in foreign currency.

Otherwise, the proposal would need Government approval through the Foreign Investment Promotion Board (FIPB).

Investors coming through the automatic route are required to file relevant documents with the Reserve Bank of India within 30 days after the issue of shares to foreign investors. Proposals which do not fulfil the condition for automatic approval require the approval of the Government.

6.8 Conclusion

The opening up of the insurance sector is expected to lead to increased competition and innovations in financial products. The size of the insurance sector, which stagnated around 0.6 percent of GDP during the 1980s and the 1990s, has accelerated in recent years as the existing insurers endeavoured to retain their market share, while new players attempted to establish themselves. Insurance products compete with other saving products such as bank term deposits and small savings. Many of the new insurance products, especially unit-linked insurance/pension schemes, now bear a close resemblance to mutual funds. While the yield on the insurance products, in the range of 7.15 per cent to 9.46 per cent during the 1990s, was normally much lower than other long-term investments, this was compensated by the insurance cover and tax benefits. As new players join the fray, the competition in respect of various financial products is expected to go up in the near future.

The key policy challenge required at the current stage is to ensure the financial stability of the new insurers, while at the same time encouraging entrepreneurship, product innovation and increasing insurance penetration especially in rural and semi-urban areas.

Presently, insurers are mainly offering insurance schemes, which are based on assured returns. This is fraught with serious risks, especially when interest rate scenario/market condition changes. In order to stave off the risks associated with assured returns schemes, insurers need to shift to unit-linked insurance schemes based on the market rates of return. While the joint ventures formed by new insurers with entities, including banks and NBFCs having a large branch/dealer network, minimise establishment costs, the contagion risks also get amplified in the process. This would require close co-ordination among the regulating agencies.

Note

1. Government of India, Planning Commission, Ninth Five Year Plan (1997-2002), Vol. I, p. 146.

7

Educational Services

7.1 Introduction

Over the decades, literacy rates have shown a substantial improvement. The total literacy rate which was only 18.33 per cent in 1951 rose to 52.21 per cent in 1991 and further increased to 65.4 per cent in 2001. According to the Census of India, 2001, the literacy rate has gone up to 75.85 per cent for males and 54.16 per cent for females. Female literacy rate has shown much higher growth, increasing by 14.87 percentage points as against 11.72 for males thus reducing the male-female differential in literacy rates from 24.84 in 1991 to 21.7 in 2001 (Table 7.1).

Table 7.1: Literacy Rates in India (1951-2001)

Census Year	Persons	Males	Females	Male-Female gap in literacy rate
1951	18.33	27.16	8.66	18.30
1961	28.30	40.40	15.35	25.05
1971	34.45	45.96	21.97	23.98
1981	43.57	56.38	29.76	26.62
1991	52.21	64.13	39.29	24.84
2001	65.38	75.85	54.16	21.70

Source: Census of India.

The Constitutional (93rd Amendment) Bill, passed by both Houses of Parliament, received the President's Assent on December 12, 2002. This was a significant measure for achieving the goal of Education for All (EFA) by making free and compulsory elementary education a fundamental right for all children in the age group of 6-14 years. In order to fulfil this constitutional obligation, Sarva Shiksha Abhiyan was launched in partnership with the States. The programme is an effort towards recognition of the need for improving the performance of the school system through a community owned approach and ensuring quality elementary education in a mission mode to all children in the age group of 6-14 years by 2010. It also seeks to bridge gender and social gaps. This programme will subsume all existing programmes (except Mahila Samakhya and Mid-day Meal Schemes) including externally aided programmes in due course with its overall framework with district as the unit of programmes implementation.

Within the education sector, elementary education has been given the highest priority in terms of sub-sectoral allocations and a number of schemes launched by the Central Government to meet the needs of the educationally disadvantaged. These have included the following.

- Operation Blackboard.
- District Primary Education Programme.
- Education Guarantee Scheme.
- Alternative and Innovative Education.
- Mahila Samakhya.
- National Programmes of Nutritional Support to Primary Education.
- Lok Jumbish.
- Shiksh Karmi Project.
- Janashala Programme.
- Pradhan Mantri Gramodaya Yojana.

The National Literacy Mission (NLM) seeks to achieve full literacy i.e. a sustainable threshold level of 75 per cent literacy by 2005. The Total Literacy Campaign (TLC) has been the principal strategy of National Literacy Mission for eradication of illiteracy in the target group. These campaigns are area-specific, time-bound, volunteer-based, cost effective and outcome-oriented. They are implemented by Zila

Saksharata Samities and district level literacy societies.

Keeping pace with its endeavours, campaigns and programmes, the NLM has strengthened and revitalized the States Literacy Missions. State Literacy Missions have been imparted greater autonomy. They now have the authority to plan, implement and monitor literacy programmes and sanction continuing education programmes at the State level. The NLM has also come to recognize the great potential that NGOs have in furthering its programmes and schemes. Given the major role, NGOs are now allowed to receive funds from Zila Sakshara Samities and actually run continuing education centres. The Jan Shikshan Sansthans have expanded their outreach and are also catering to the rural segment by offering around 225 vocational training courses.

7.2 Elementary Education

Some select programmes for elementary education are described below.

District Primary Education Programme: Launched in 1994 in 42 districts, this is a Centrally Sponsored scheme aiming at providing access to primary education for all children, reducing primary dropout rates to less than 10 percent, increasing learning achievement of primary school students by at least 25 per cent and reducing gender and social groups to less than 5 per cent.

National Programme of Nutritional Support to Primary Education: Launched on 15th August 1995 with the objective to boost the Universalisation of Primary Education by impacting upon enrolment, attendance, retention and nutritional needs of children studying in class I–V. Under this programme more than 10 crore children are being targeted for coverage. At present, Gujarat, Kerala, Tamil Nadu, Madhya Pradesh, Chattisgarh, Orissa, Karnataka and Delhi are providing cooked meals. The remaining States and UTs are distributing foodgrains (wheat/rice).

Pradhan Mantri Gramodaya Yojana: This programme was

launched during 2000-01 and envisages Additional Central Assistance for basic minimum services in certain priority areas. The scheme has six components covering elementary education, primary health, rural shelter, rural drinking water, nutrition and rural electrification. A minimum of 10 per cent of ACA for all components except nutrition (for which it is 15 per cent) has been fixed. The allocation for the remaining 35 per cent of ACA would be decided by the States and UTs among the components of the Scheme, as per their priorities. Funds for elementary education sector under PMGY are utilized to further the goal of Universalisation of Elementary Education.

Sarva Shiksha Abhiyan (SSA): The main vehicle for providing elementary education to all children is the ongoing comprehensive programme called Sarva Siksha Abhiyan (SSA) launched in 2001-02. The goals of SSA are the following.

- All children in School, Education Guarantee Centre, Alternate School, Back-to-School camp by 2005.
- Bridge all gender and social category gaps at the primary stage by 2007 and at elementary education level by 2010.
- Universal retention by 2010.
- Focus on elementary education of satisfactory quality with emphasis on education for life.

SSA, implemented in partnership with the States, addresses the needs of 209 million children in the age group of 6-14 years. It covers 9.72 lakh existing primary and upper primary schools and 36.95 lakh teachers.

National Programme for Education of Girls at Elementary Level (NPEGEL): It is an important component of SSA. NPEGEL provides additional support by way of girl-child friendly schools, stationery, uniforms, etc. for girls' education in educationally backward blocks (EBB), and in other areas for elementary education of under privileged and disadvantaged sections. EBBs are blocks with female literacy below, and gender gap above, the national average. Apart from EBBs,

NPEGEL is also implemented in blocks of districts which are not covered under EBBs but have at least 5 per cent SC/ST population and where SC/ST female literacy is below 10 per cent, and also in select urban slums. In the Tenth Five Year Plan, an amount of Rs.1064.80 crore has been earmarked for this programme.

Education Guarantee Scheme and Alternative and Innovative Education (EGS&AIE): Another important component of SSA is the EGS&AIE. It is specially designed to provide access to elementary education to children in school-less habitations and out-of-school children. It supports flexible strategies for out-of-school children through bridge courses, residential camps, drop-in centres, summer camps, remedial coaching, etc., and helped to provide elementary education to 85.67 lakh children in 2004-05.

Mid-Day Meal Scheme: The Centrally-sponsored Mid-Day Meal Scheme was revised and universalized at primary level with effect from September, 2004 to make a provision for providing cooked meals to children studying in Government, Government-aided, and local body schools and EGS&AIE centres. Besides providing foodgrains free of cost to the States/UTs, and foodgrains transportation subsidy, the Central Government provides assistance for converting foodgrains into cooked meal at a rate of Re. 1 per child per day. The programme now covers nearly 12 crore children studying in over 9 lakh primary schools and EGS&AIE Centres. Budget provision for this scheme, which is the world's largest school feeding programme involving preparation of a hot meal everyday, for 2005-06 is Rs. 3,345 crore.

Kasturba Gandhi Balika Vidyalaya (KGBV): The KGBV scheme was launched in August, 2004 to set up 750 residential schools at elementary level for girls belonging predominantly to the SC, ST, OBC and minorities, in EBBs. All 750 KGBVs have now been sanctioned by the Government of India, with 117 KGBVs (15.6 per cent) allocated to blocks with substantial minority population. Budget provision for the scheme for 2005-06 is Rs. 250 crore.

Prarambhik Shiksha Kosh (PSK): Department of Elementary Education and Literacy issued orders on November 14, 2005 constituting Prarambhik Shiksha Kosh (PSK) to receive the proceeds of the education cess imposed through Finance (No.2) Act, 2004. PSK is a separate, dedicated, non-lapsable fund to be maintained by the Ministry of Human Resource Development.

In education, the elementary sector is besieged by numerous systemic problems such as inadequate school infrastructure, presence of single-teacher schools, high teacher absenteeism (especially in rural areas), large-scale teacher vacancies, inadequate equipment, etc. This brings into focus the role of decentralization and people's participation in the provision of basic services. It is essential that control over schools and teachers should be transferred to local bodies, having a direct interest in teacher performance. This has also been highlighted as an area of emphasis in the Tenth Plan.

The National Policy on Education (NPE), 1986, as modified in 1992, emphasized three aspects in relation to elementary education.

- Universal access and enrolment.
- Universal retention of children up to 14 years of age.
- A substantial improvement in the quality of education to enable all children to achieve essential levels of learning.

NPE emphasized that education must play a positive and interventionist role in correcting social and regional imbalance, empowering women, and in securing a rightful place for the disadvantaged and the minorities. Government is firmly committed to providing education for all, the priority areas being free and compulsory elementary education, covering children with special needs, eradication of illiteracy, education for women's equality, and special focus on the education of SCs/STs and Minorities.

Allocation for elementary education in the Tenth Five Year Plan period (2002-07) at Rs. 28,750 crore was 75 per cent higher than the allocation in the Ninth Plan. Resources for elementary education have been augmented through imposition of the education cess at the rate of 2 per cent on direct and indirect Central taxes imposed through Finance (No.2) Act, 2004. With the imposition of the education cess, budgeted outlay for elementary and adult education more than doubled from Rs. 6,000 crore in 2004-05 to Rs. 12,532 crore in 2005-06.

7.3 Secondary and Higher Education

Secondary Education sector prepares students in the age group of 14-18 years for entry into higher education as well as for the world of work. The Kendriya Vidyalaya Sangathan manages 849 Kendriya Vidyalaya (as on December 31, 2001). The Navodaya Vidyalaya Samiti, through more than 451 institutions in predominantly rural areas, has taken up activities for extension of infrastructural facilities, introduction of vocational courses, training of teachers etc.

Women belonging to SC and ST and those living in rural areas are the most disadvantaged. A Constitution Amendment Bill was passed by Parliament in December, 2005, which enables the State to make special provisions, by law, for admission of students belonging to SC, ST and socially and educationally backward classes to educational institutions, including aided and unaided private educational institutions, except minority institutions referred to in Article 30(1) of the Constitution.

7.4 Technical Education

Technical and professional education in the country has played a significant role in economic and technical development by producing quality manpower. There are at present 1,203 approved engineering colleges at the degree and 1,195 colleges at the diploma level. Apart from this, 1,006 institutes impart courses on Master of Computer Application (MCA).

There are 930 approved Management Institutes imparting

MBA courses. From the current academic year, All India Council for Technical Education (AICTE) has delegated the powers of approval of Diploma level technical institutes to the State Governments. Strong linkages have developed between technical institutions and the industry. For strengthening technical education and improving the quality of polytechnic pass outs, various steps have been taken through Technical Education Development programmes.

7.5 Adult Education

Literacy rates in India have risen sharply from 18.3 per cent in 1951 to 64.8 per cent in 2001. Nevertheless, India continues to lag behind several other developing countries in the region such as China (86 per cent) and Sri Lanka (92 per cent). The National Literacy Mission (NLM) was launched on May 5, 1988 as a Technology Mission to impart functional literacy to non-literates in the country in the age group of 15-35 years in a time-bound manner. This age-group has been the focus of attention because they are in the productive and reproductive period of life. The NPE,1986, as modified in 1992, recognizes the NLM as one of the three instruments to eradicate illiteracy from the country, the other two being SSA and non-formal education.

NLM's objective is to attain a sustainable threshold literacy rate of 75 per cent by 2007. The Total Literacy Campaign (TLC) has been the principal strategy of National Literacy Mission for eradication of illiteracy in the target age-group. These campaigns implemented by Zila Saksharata Samities (District Level Literacy Societies) are area-specific, time-bound, volunteer-based, cost effective and outcome-oriented.

At present, 137 districts are implementing TLCs, 165 districts Post Literacy Programmes and 295 districts Continuing Education Programmes. In addition, 157 Jan Shikshan Sansthan have been set up to provide vocational training to the neo-literates and backward sections of the society, and 25 State Resource Centres established for providing academic and technical resource support for thc literacy programmes.

NLM has accorded priority for the promotion of female literacy. According to 2001 Census, 47 districts in the country have female literacy rate below 30 percent. Most of these districts are concentrated in Bihar, Jharkhand, Uttar Pradesh and Orissa. Special innovative projects have been taken up to raise the level of female literacy in these areas. Special efforts have been made to target female Panchayati Raj functionaries and make them literate.

Out of 600 districts in the country 587 have since been covered under Adult Education Programmes. At present 174 districts are in progress under Total Literacy Campaigns, 212 under Post Literacy Programmes and 201 under Continuing Education Programme. About 96.69 million persons have been made literate as on 31.3.2002. Out of the total clientele group under different Adult Education Schemes, about 60 percent of the beneficiaries are women, while 22 percent and 12 per cent belong to scheduled castes and scheduled tribes respectively. Besides, 108 Jan Shikshan Sansthans and 25 State Resource Centres are functioning. The Directorate of Adult Education is functioning as National Resource Centre.

7.6 Promoting Skill Development

Virtually every service sub-sector in the country is experiencing a severe shortage of skilled personnel on account of the booming conditions prevailing in service economy during the past few years. Shortages persist not only at the level of managers and supervisors but also at the level of skilled workmen in most sub-sectors. Thus in healthcare there is a shortage of not only doctors and nurses but also of radiographers and laboratory technicians; in the hospitality sector there is dearth of hotel managers as well as of cooks and waiters; in IT and BPO services we need not only software specialists but also simple graduates with some amount of fluency in the English language. In many cases the products of existing education and vocational training institutions are not fit for employment without undergoing further training while in others there is shortage of educational and training facilities. Expansion of technical and higher education and improvement in its quality will take care of some of the shortages but the vocational training requirements of the services sector need to be systematically addressed and given impetus through government initiative.

7.7 Reforming Education

It is widely acknowledged that the education system in India is woefully inadequate for the social and economic development of the country in general and for enhancing the competitiveness of the services sector in particular. The goal of bringing all children in the age group 6-14 to schools is still unrealised although the number of out-of-school children has been brought down from 32 million in 2001-02 to 7.1 million in July 2006. Although a great deal of progress has been made under the Sarva Shiksha Abhiyan the quality of education at the primary level still lags behind. Students need more than eight years education to acquire the skills needed for the services market and secondary education is the minimum needed for this purpose.

For developing a knowledge economy, we have to build further on the base of secondary education and give attention to improvement of both quality and quantity of higher education.

Recent decades have seen the emergence of private sector institutions particularly in technical education financed by large capitation fees charged by them. This development has been inequitable, as it has led to the deprivation of a large number of students who have not been able to pay the substantial sums involved in the capitation fees. While encouraging private sector initiative to expand higher education it has become necessary for the Government to ensure that private sector institutions take measures to provide scholarships and free-ships to an adequate number of meritorious students (and those from historically disadvantaged and vulnerable groups) who do not have the means to pay the fees.

One of the main reasons for falling standards of higher education is the teacher shortage in the institutions of higher learning, particularly the technical education institutions. The salaries commanded by graduates in the market are so high that they do not have the motivation to move on for post-graduation or doctoral level with the ultimate objective of becoming teachers. In order to make the teaching profession attractive and motivate bright young professionals to take post-graduate courses, it is necessary to look at the salary structure and career opportunities of teachers in colleges. Research project funds must be shared as incentive payment to the faculty and the faculty should be given maximum freedom to undertake consultancies.

The decline in standards in higher education is also due to the failure to revise the curricula to keep pace with the developments in the various fields of knowledge as well in the society. The curricula must be revised every three years and the revisions must be subjected to outside peer review. The process of revision should be streamlined and decentralised with more autonomy given to teachers.

One of the major reforms needed in the education system is a change in the method of assessment of students, which relies exclusively on examinations. The current system is inadequate because it tests memory rather than understanding and dose not encourage the development of analytical and creative abilities. Assessment of students must be based on the work done throughout the year rather than being judged solely on the performance during the annual examination. Evaluation of courses and teachers by students should also be used as an input in the process of assessment of students. Semester system must be introduced in the institutions of higher education. Also important is the need to introduce a system of credits whereby a student who discontinues studies or who changes institutions may be granted recognition for the courses completed earlier, thus granting them spatial and temporal flexibility in pursuing studies.

The main instrument used by the UGC to obtain improvement in the standards of teaching in institutions of higher education is to require them to adhere to minimum standards in infrastructure and physical facilities and human resources as a condition for financial assistance. However, what is needed is to induce them to be for ever striving to undertake self-improvement on a voluntary basis to obtain better standards. With this end in view in1994 the UGC established the National Assessment and Accreditation Council (NAAC) to undertake accreditation of institutions desirous of undertaking such improvement. Unfortunately the response has not been satisfactory and up to 2007 only 130 out of 367 universities and 3381 out of 18000 colleges have been accredited. It is necessary to promote the process of accreditation by making available additional discretionary funds to the funding agencies to be utilised for the purpose.

The educational institutions are regulated by the UGC and a number of Councils such as the All India Council for Technical Education (AICTE), the Medical Council of India (MCI) etc. The Councils have their own rules and regulations and there is a large overlap of their functions with that of the UGC. It has become imperative to restructure the apex level bodies in order to streamline their functioning. There is also an acute need for reform in the structures of governance of universities. The size and composition of University Courts, Academic Councils and Executive Councils slows down decision making processes. These bodies and the Vice Chancellors are unable to function harmoniously. It is necessary to establish smaller Standing Councils of academic councils for meeting frequently and taking expeditious decisions.

8

Transport and Communication Services

8.1 Transport Services

An efficient transport system is a pre-requisite for sustained economic development. It is not only the key infrastructural input for the growth process but also plays a significant role in promoting national integration, which is particularly important in a large country like India. In a liberalized set-up, an efficient transport network becomes all the more important in order to increase productivity and enhance the competitive efficiency of the economy in the world market. The transport system also plays an important role in promoting the development of the backward regions and integrating them with the mainstream economy by opening them to trade and investment.

8.1.1 Indian Railways: Indian Railways, with a capital base of about Rs. 55,000 crore, is the principal mode of transportation for carrying bulk freight and long distance passenger traffic. Given India's continental size, geography, resource endowment and diversity, the Railways play a key role in not only meeting the transport needs of the country, but also in binding together dispersed areas, thus, promoting national integration. It also plays a key role during war and emergencies when huge quantities of material and men are required to be moved across the country at short notice.

Indian Railways has historically played an important integrating role in the social and economic development of the country. It has an extensive network which is spread over 63,140 Route Kilometre (RKm), comprising Broad Gauge (45,099 RKm), Metre Gauge (14,776 RKm) and Narrow Gauge (3,265 RKm). Approximately, 25 per cent of the network is electrified.

Being a public utility service, Indian Railways has been undertaking certain uneconomical operations in the larger social and national interests, so as to provide affordable transport facilities to the common man and to carry certain essential commodities meant for mass consumption at very low freight rates. This is termed as Social Service Obligation. The losses incurred on passenger services are cross-subsidized by profit earned through freight services as also earnings from higher classes of passenger travel. In addition, cross-subsidization exists within the freight services since certain commodities, such as salt, fruits, vegetables etc. are being carried at much below cost of operations.

In the absence of any subsidy from the government to fulfil such Social Service Obligation, the level of cross-subsidization can only be reduced through proper tariff rationalization. The Railways are also making efforts to close down uneconomic branch lines where alternative modes of transport exist or can be developed.

On August 15, 2002, the Prime Minister approved an important initiative to put Indian Railways on the path of fast track growth. The Government has drawn up an important non-budgetary investment initiative for the development of Indian Railways to be called the National Rail Vikas Yojana. Salient features of this scheme are the following.

- Capacity bottlenecks in the critical sections of the railway network will be removed at an investment of Rs. 15,000 crore over the next five years, i.e. during the Tenth Plan period (2002-07).
- Strengthening of the Golden Quadrilateral and its Diagonals to enable the Railways to run more long-distance mail/express trains and freight trains at a higher speed of 100 kmph at a cost of Rs. 8,000 crore.
- Strengthening of rail connectivity to ports and development of multimodal corridors to hinterland at a cost of Rs. 3,000 crore.
- Construction of four mega bridges – two over River

Ganga, one over River Brahmaputra, and one over River Kosi, at a cost of Rs. 3,500 crore.

- Accelerated completion of last mile and other important projects at a cost of Rs. 763 crore.
- Completion of all viable Sanctioned Railway Projects within the next 10 years.
- 'Operation Cleanliness' to significantly improve the standards of sanitation at railway stations, on platforms and inside railway compartments.

There is need for a strategic shift in the objectives of the Railways so that it can regain some of the market it has lost over the past few decades to other competing modes of transport. In the light of massive investment taking place in the highway and pipeline sectors, the Railways must reorient their objectives in order to cope with a more competitive market. Indian Railways will have to become more user-friendly and market-savvy organization, which responds quickly to customer needs.

The thrust has to be on modernization and technological upgradation of the Railway system, particularly along the Golden Quadrangle and its diagonals. With a view to augmenting its capacity and improving the safety and reliability of railway services, the Indian Railways need to run primarily on commercial lines. While it should continue to play its social and developmental role, it should be suitably compensated for such services. At the same time, Railways need to shed those activities which are not connected to the core business of passengers and freight.

One of the contributing factors for the decline in the financial fortunes of Indian Railways is the loss of freight market share. Freight has been the key earner for Railways. The Railways cannot afford to continue the historical rate of growth of 3-4 per cent in freight traffic movement and needs to pursue a high growth rate. Otherwise, not only will the Indian Railways get marginalised but this would also lead to an economic slowdown due to infrastructural bottlenecks.

In order to increase its market share, the Railways has to improve the quality of its services. Door-to-door service through the process of containerization with necessary road links as a part of service would provide a major boost in this regard. Reducing the time taken in delivery of goods through introduction of faster freight trains and steps towards making freight service user-friendly would help in increasing the share of Railways in freight traffic.

In short, the railways remain an extremely important area, given the fact that transportation by rail has the highest energy efficiency as compared with other options. This suggests that if the institutional mechanisms come about, then the cost of transportation by railways would be much cheaper than that of transport by road. However, this is likely to require substantial reforms in the functioning of railways. The experience with the transformation of telecom, roads and ports serve as role models for the institutional change that may be required.

8.1.2 Roads and Road Transport: Roads are the key to the development of an economy. A good road network constitutes the basic infrastructure that propels the development process through connectivity and opening up the backward regions to trade and investment. Roads also play a key role in inter-modal transport development, establishing links with airports, railway stations and ports. In addition, they have an important role in promoting national integration, which is particularly important in a large country like India.

India has an extensive road network of more than 3.3 million km making it one of the largest in the world. Roads in India, for the purpose of their management and administration are divided into the following categories.

- National highways.
- State highways.
- District roads.
- Rural roads.
- Special purpose roads (for use by military, ports etc.)

Under the Constitution, responsibility for the development

and maintenance of national highways rests with the Central Government while other roads are the responsibility of the State Government concerned.

National highways are the prime arterial routes spanning about 58,112 km throughout the country and cater to about 45 per cent of the total road transport demand. Over the years, roads have grown in prominence as a mechanism for moving goods and people in the country. This is partly reflected in greater innate flexibility of road transportation. However, this development is giving tough competition to the Indian railways.

While the national highways are intended to facilitate medium and long haul inter-city passenger and freight traffic across the country, state highways are meant to carry the traffic within the state. Together, they provide the main mobility function in the transportation system. District roads and village roads serve to connect villages to provide accessibility and market linkages. Major district roads provide the secondary function of linkages between the main roads and the rural roads.

Presently, the national highways are being developed, maintained and managed under an agency system. The overall responsibility including planning, budgeting, standardisation is handled by the Ministry of Surface Transport. The Government of India has, however, under an Act of Parliament in 1988, established the National Highways Authority of India (NHAI) for developing, maintaining and managing the national highways as a single agency. The functions relating to externally-aided projects, implementation of the policy of private sector participation and development of wayside amenities along the national highways have been assigned to NHAI.

Funds required for the national highways are provided by Central Government budgets on a yearly basis. For State Roads, funds come from by the respective state government's budget. The states are directly responsible for execution of works on State Roads and managing them. Funds for State Roads developed as strategic roads serving the requirements of defence and civilian traffic, come from the Central Government.

Being capital-intensive in nature, road construction requires huge amounts of funds. Current estimates suggest that the cost of a four-lane highway works out to roughly Rs. 4.5 crore per kilometre, and the cost of a protected access, six-lane expressway works out to roughly Rs. 8.5 crore per kilometre. As of today, the experiences with tolling suggest that there is limited scope for obtaining user charges through tolls. This has raised difficult questions about how road construction would be financed.

A key innovation in recent years has been the creation of a major new source of funding for national, state and rural roads, viz. the Central Road Fund (CRF), created under the Central Road Fund Act, 2000. This was a major milestone in obtaining user charges to fund road construction. In fact, this fund is the financial foundation of an important project: the National Highway Development Project (NHDP), which entails expansion of the existing two-lane highways to four/six lanes and strengthening of existing lanes on nearly 13,000 km. The overall project is one of the largest single highway project in the world.

The Control of National Highways (Land and Traffic) Act, 2002 was passed by Parliament and notified. The legislation aims at preventing unauthorized occupation of highway land and seeks to control access points to National Highways and regulate traffic on them. It also envisages establishment of Highway Administrations to enforce the law and setting up tribunals to hear appeals against their orders.

Pradhan Mantri Gram Sadak Yojana (PMGSY) was launched in October 2000. The primary objective of PMGSY is to provide connectivity, by way of all-weather roads, to the unconnected habitations in the rural areas, so that habitations with population of 1,000 and above are covered in three years

(2000-2003). All unconnected habitations with a population of 500 persons and above are to be covered by the end of the Tenth Plan Period (2007). In respect of the hill States (North-East, Sikkim, Himachal Pradesh, Jammu and Kashmir, Uttranchal) and the desert areas, the objective is to connect habitations with a population of 250 persons and above. The programme also aims to achieve an equitable development of the rural roads network in different States/districts so as to fully exploit the latent potential for rural growth. The PMGSY is being implemented as a 100 per cent centrally sponsored scheme.

Government has set ambitious plans for upgradation of national highways in a phased manner in the years to come. A presentation was made before the Committee on Infrastructure proposing the following projects in addition to the completion of the ongoing works included under NHDP Phase-I and Phase-II:

- 4-laning of 11,113 km (NHDP Phase-III) including 4,035 km already approved.
- Accelerated road development programme for the North Eastern region.
- 2-laning with paved shoulders of 20,000 km of national highways (NHDP Phase-IV).
- 6-laning of GQ and some other selected stretches covering 6,500 km (NHDP Phase-V).
- Development of 1,000 km of express ways (NHDP Phase-VI).
- Development of ring roads, bypasses, grade separators, service roads etc. (NHDP Phase-VII).

As a policy, Government has decided to take up future phases of NHDP proposals mainly on a PPP basis. Implementation of projects through construction contracts will be only in exceptional cases where private sector participation is not possible at all.

8.1.3 Ports: Although endowed with a strategic location in the Indian Ocean and an extensive coastline, India has not emerged as a forerunner in maritime activities. This has been due to several reasons including her conscious policy of self-reliance through import substitution and lack of adequate thrust on export promotion.

However, in the post-1991 era, India has started to reach out and partake in the windfall that globalisation has brought in its wake. The upgradation and expansion of ports is vital to strengthen India's position in world trade and to handle the growing volume of international trade.

Ports are an important component of infrastructure. There are 12 major and 184 minor and intermediate ports in India which service the Indian coastline. Major ports handle about 75 per cent of port traffic while minor ports handle the remaining.

The major ports are Chennai, Cochin, Ennore, Kandla, Kolkata, Mormugao, Mumbai, New Mangalore, Paradip, Tutocorin and Visakhapatnam. The minor ports are located in Gujarat (40), Maharashtra (53), Goa (5), Daman & Diu (2), Karnataka (9), Kerala (13), Lakshadweep (10), Tamil Nadu (14), Pondicherry (1) Andhra Pradesh (12), Orissa (2) and Andaman & Nicobar (23).

The primary responsibility for development and management of major ports rests with the Central Government. These ports are governed by the Major Port Trusts Act, 1963, which enables them to conduct regulatory as well as commercial functions.

State governments administer intermediate and the minor ports under the Indian Ports Act, 1908, which delineates the regulatory powers of the Port Authority.

The other Acts applicable to the port sector are the Merchant Shipping Act, 1958, which describes the powers of the regulatory authority, i.e. the Director General, Shipping.

The Dock Workers (Regulation and Employment) Act, 1948, and Dock Workers (Safety Health and Welfare) Act of 1986 regulate the conditions of employment, service and other matters relating to dock workers.

Each major port has a Board of Trustees representing various interests connected with port operations and the shipping industry. The Chairman of each major Port Trust is appointed by the Central Government. Besides the Chairman, who is usually an IAS officer, the Port Trust Board comprises of the Deputy Chairman (usually from the port cadre) and representatives of customs, railways, defence, state government, ship owners, shippers, labour etc. Apart from the Chairman and Deputy Chairman, all others are part-time members.

A. Problems Faced by Indian Ports: The key problem faced by Indian ports is low productivity. The major factors that have led to this can be identified as follows:

- Operational constraints such as frequent breakdown of cargo-handling equipment due to obsolescence or wrong specification of equipment, poor maintenance etc.
- Inadequate facilities for dredging of berth and channels at certain ports and inadequacy of container handling facilities.
- Inefficient and non-operational deployment of port equipment.
- Labour intensive methods of bulk handling of sensitive commodities like thermal coal.
- Poor inter-departmental communication especially between Customs and Port Authorities.

Recent policy measures have ushered in new institutional arrangements and have yielded results in terms of measurable outcomes such as the delays at ports. While performance metrics have improved considerably, they continue to lag international standards. Private investment in the sector has been mainly from captive users, and these port terminals now compare well with international norms at efficiency.

For the purpose of attracting private sector investment, model bid documents have been prepared laying down transparent bidding procedure, including qualifications and selection criteria.

Traditionally, all over the world, the ownership of ports has been dominated by the public sector. But privatization of port facilities and services has now gathered momentum and India is also following the trend and an enabling policy framework has already been put in place. Depending on the nature of facility/service, private operators can enter into a service contract, a management contract, a concession agreement or a divestiture to operate port services. Areas that have been opened up to the private sector on a BOT basis include construction of cargo handling berths and dry-docks, container terminals and warehousing facilities and ship repair facilities.

The broad objectives of the participation of private sector in port development have been to bring about an improvement in efficiency, productivity, quality of service as well as to usher competitiveness in the provision of port services. In addition, the private sector is expected to mobilize adequate resources required for capacity augmentation and introduce the latest technology and management techniques in the port sector.

The Government has identified the following areas for private sector participation:

- Leasing out assets of the ports.
- Construction and operation of container terminals, multiple cargo berths and specialized cargo berths, warehousing, storage facilities, tank farms, container freight stations, setting up of captive power plants etc.
- Leasing of equipment for cargo handling and leasing of floating rafts from the private sector.
- Pilotage.
- Captive facilities for port based industries.

The major ports urgently need to upgrade their handling technology modernise their equipment and management and raise adequate resources, both for the creation of additional port facilities and to improve existing ones. This demands a complete new approach. Ports worldwide have used commercialisation, liberalization, privatisation, and modernisation of port administration as strategies to deal with these issues.

It is quite feasible to raise the required resources. However, this will require adoption of innovative methods. Autonomous port authorities should operate on commercial lines so they can raise resources from the primary market by way of equity and debt and from FIs. On the basis of the existing tariff levels, it should be possible for the port authorities to service debt obligations and pay a reasonable return to investors on equity.

There is urgent need to delegate adequate powers to the Port Trusts to facilitate the speedy creation and operation of assets. Projects to be executed through private participation involving no investment by the ports should not require the approval of the expenditure Finance Committee. Qualitative improvement in port infrastructure cannot be achieved without some sort of autonomy to the ports and expanding them to competition by way of private sector participation for various cargo handling activities.

Indian ports will have to upgrade their technology levels to be comparable to international standards. In the modernised ports, cargo would be mechanically handled; there should be special facilities for handling container and bulk cargo and computer based cargo clearance including customer clearance.

Labour resistance is perceived as a primary impediment to greater private sector participation. The government must deal with this as a priority issue as this is a critical barrier to overcome in any privatization process. Modernisation and restructuring of ports are to be considered as a continuous process for reallocating productive assets, labour, capital and management. The process of restructuring and modernisation would essentially involve a shift to a better management and change in a worker's job description. This would require upgradation of the worker's skills in line with new needs.

Port authorities also need to take up area rejuvenation

programmes. Indian ports have large tracts of urban land which could be optimally utilised for facilitating the required restructuring. This would require an integrated and comprehensive approach and possibly an appropriate institutional mechanism.

The existing system of labour compensation too needs a relook. It may be advisable to move from a monolithic pay structure to piece-based wage structure. This would set up an incentive system which would increase efficiency and innovation at the lowest level.

Ports being strategic assets, privatization of certain services of ports needs consideration. Ports perform multifarious activities. These include cargo handling, storage, warehousing, customs clearance, security and administration. Each of these activities could be considered as separate profit centres and appropriate policies should be evolved for commercialisation and private sector participation in each case. It may be better to make the ports work as corporate entities with administrative independence and the ability to raise finances for development.

In conclusion, a key insight in the area of ports has been the extent to which existing port facilities can yield better output given the better institutional mechanisms, without requiring substantial new investments. There are important experiments currently taking place across the country in terms of new contractual structures. They have already yielded results in terms of giving a sharp improvement as compared to the state of ports in India during the pre-reforms period. However, the performance of ports in India still lags far behind the standards seen in ports such as Singapore or Hong Kong. Looking forward, the key question that requires focus is establishment of a framework through which there is competition between multiple operators in a given port, and competition between ports.

8.1.4 Civil Aviation: The main advantage of civil aviation vis-à-vis railways and road transport is the speed of travel and consequent saving of time. A part of this gain is, however, nullified for short-haul flights due to time taken in reporting, security checks, flying, luggage clearance etc. Air travel, nevertheless, retains a substantial edge over other modes of transport for long distance travel. It is particularly useful for business travel, international tourism and for transporting high value and perishable commodities. Air transport also provides easy accessibility to remote regions, which has implications for national integration and security. The advantage, however, has to be weighed against high cost of air travel and cost to the economy because of its high fuel intensity.

The civil aviation sector has plays an important role in India's economy. It provides fast and reliable mode of transport across the country and is particularly important for many areas/places still not adequately connected by rail or road. With increasing globalization, this sector will play a more significant role in integrating the Indian economy with the rest of the world.

The civil aviation sector could broadly be divided into three distinct functional entities: (a) regulatory-cum-developmental, (b) operational and (c) infrastructural.

The regulatory functions are the responsibility of the Directorate General of Civil Aviation (DGCA) and Bureau of Civil Aviation Security (BCAS).

Operational functions are performed by Air India Ltd., Indian Airlines Ltd., Pawan Hans Helicopters Ltd. together with other private sector airline operators. Air India provides international air services while Indian Airlines and its wholly-owned subsidiary, Alliance Air, and other operators provide domestic air services in the country. Indian Airlines also provides international air services to some of the neighbouring countries. Pawan Hans Helicopters provides helicopter support services primarily in the petroleum sector.

Infrastructural facilities are provided by the Airports Authority of India (AAI). It manages 94 civil airports including 11 international airports at Delhi, Mumbai, Kolkata, Chennai, Thiruvananthapuram, Bangalore, Hyderabad, Ahmedabad, Goa, Amritsar and Guwahati and 28 civil enclaves at defence airfields. The Indira Gandhi Rashtriya Udan Academy (IGRUA) is the premier flying training for the award of the commercial pilots licence and commercial helicopter pilots licence. Hotel Corporation of India, a subsidiary of Air India Ltd., is in the business of providing in-flight catering.

It is now increasingly recognized that aviation, far from being a mere mode of transportation for a small elite group, makes an important contribution to the national economy and is crucial for sustainable development of trade and tourism. The civil aviation sector has made significant strides in coping with the growth of international and domestic traffic. This sector provides three categories of services, viz. operational, infrastructure and regulatory-cum-developmental.

The monopoly of public sector air carriers ended with the amendment of Air Corporation Act, 1953 in March, 1994. Automatic approval for foreign equity participation in airport infrastructure up to 100 per cent has been allowed. Foreign equity up to 40 per cent and investment by Non-resident Indians up to 100 per cent is also permitted. Equity from foreign airlines is not allowed in domestic air-transport services directly or indirectly. Foreign Financial Institutions allowed to hold equity in the domestic air-transport sector provided they do not have foreign airlines as their shareholders.

Foreign investors are allowed to have representation (up to 33 per cent of total) on Board of Directors of the domestic airline company. Government is considering private sector participation, construction and operation of new airports on a BOT basis.

Domestic air services are provided by Indian Airlines and private airlines (scheduled and non-scheduled). International air services are handled by Air India. Pawan Hans Helicopters provides helicopter support services to the petroleum sector including ONGC and OIL India Ltd. and connects remote and inaccessible areas of the North-Eastern region and islands of the country. It also provides air support services to several customers including State and Union Territory Governments, public sector undertakings and private sector companies. Infrastructure facilities are taken care of by the Airports Authority of India.

The development of airports in the country is no longer in the domain of public sector. The Airport Infrastructure Policy, 1997, permits private equity participation in development of airport infrastructure. Success has been achieved in developing green-field airport in the country. With the initiative of State Government of Kerala, a new international airport has been constructed and commissioned at Cochin. The project has been financed from contributions from Non-Resident Indians and loan from financial institutions. The airport is being managed by Cochin International Airport Ltd. in which the State Government holds majority shareholdings.

The international airport in Delhi and Mumbai are being modernized and upgraded through private sector participation. In the Joint Venture (JV), AAI and other Government PSU will be holding 26 per cent equity. The balance 74 per cent will be held by the strategic partner. FDI in this transaction has been capped at 49 per cent. Towards this end, Expressions of Interest (EOI) were invited and bidders were short listed. AAI had issued Request for Proposal (RFP) to selected Pre-Qualified Bidders (PQBs) on April 1, 2005. On the basis of the evaluation of Technical and Financial Bids, the private partners for modernization and development of Delhi and Mumbai airports were selected.

Construction work at greenfield airports of international standards at Hyderabad and Bangalore has commenced. The two airports are likely to be operational by the middle of the year 2008. 'In-principle' approval has already been granted to set up a similar greenfield airport in Goa. In-principle approval has been obtained to build new international terminals at Ahmedabad and Trivandrum airports. State Governments are encouraged to set up greenfield airports with private sector participation. Proposals to set up Greenfield airports in Navi Mumbai, Kannur in Kerala, Ladhowal near Ludhiana and Pakyong near Gangtok in Sikkim are in the pipeline. An international greenfield airport has already been built and is operational in Kochi.

Airport Authority of India (AAI) is also considering development of non-metro airports. Indian Financial Consultants (IFC) and Global Technical Advisers have been appointed for ten airports, namely Ahmedabad, Amritsar, Goa, Guwahati, Lucknow, Madurai, Jaipur, Mangalore, Trivandrum and Udaipur. The technoeconomic feasibility study (TEFS) have been received for all the 10 non-metro airports from GTA and IFC. The works pertaining to these 10 non-metro airports are being taken up by AAI in a phased manner. The terminal building and associated infrastructure like car park/roads and air side work, with an estimated cost of Rs. 1,437 crore for Phase I (2006-08), will be taken up by AAI. The land use plans recommended by GTA/IFC for enhancement of non-aeronautical revenue will be restricted to passenger-related services or related to Aircraft Services or Air Traffic Services as per provisions of the AAI Act and State Government/Local body bye laws.

In addition to these 10 non-metro airports, AAI has identified 15 more non-metro airports, namely, Agatti, Aurangabad, Bhopal, Bhubaneswar, Coimbatore, Indore, Khajuraho, Nagpur, Patna, Port Blair, Rajkot, Trichy, Vadodra, Varanasi and Vizag, for development. For carrying out TEFS for each of these 15 airports, the process for appointment of GTA and IFC is nearing completion. Five more airports, namely Agartala, Dehradun, Imphal, Ranchi, and Raipur, have been identified for carrying out the TEFS, and for which process for appointment of GTA is being initiated. The consultants will identify the viable development works, specific to each airport. The approximate cost of development of these non-metro airports is estimated to be of the order of Rs. 5,000 crore.

8.2 Telecommunications

The telecommunications sector has undergone a total transformation throughout the world over the last two decades. Technological advances have revolutionised the quality and range of services available. Moreover, developments in the sphere of information technology, satellite-based television broadcasting, new forms of communication such as data communication through e-mail and associated services through the internet, are transforming the way people communicate and conduct business.

Clearly, a country's ability to benefit from this revolution depends heavily on the modernity of its telecommunications network. Countries that can acquire and access information on demand and then integrate them usefully into their industrial structure through a modern telecommunications network are most likely to experience high rates of growth. Large-scale use of information and telecommunications technologies directly influences productivity, cost effectiveness and competitiveness in industries with high levels of product differentiation and low levels of unit prices. In these industries, prompt availability of information about demand trends or price movements can boost competitive advantage. International competitiveness of the textile, garment, toy and consumer electronics industries in Taiwan and the Philippines have been found to be effective due to advanced telecommunications services that allow tight links between commercial distribution in American and European markets and local production.

An advanced telecommunications system is equally important for service industries like banking, trading, retailing, transportation, maintenance and insurance where information and real-time communication are vital to the production process. A reduction in the costs of these services will indirectly enhance international competitiveness within the entire economic system, since lower marketing costs mean lower costs for manufacturing firms exposed to international trade. The extraordinary efficiency of financial markets of Hong Kong and Singapore is based on the extensive use of such advanced telecommunications services.

Thus, improved communication is vital for productivity in all spheres of activity: agriculture, industry, trade and commerce. In addition, with the increasing movement of people within and outside the country, easy communication is essential for enhancing human welfare so that families, friends and acquaintances can overcome the barriers of distance. For a developing economy like India, it is thus important that policies and programmes be initiated, and resources committed to bring about rapid growth in the sector.

In operation since 1851, Indian telecommunications is among the oldest such systems in the world. Telephone services in the country were originally operated by private companies which were taken over by the Government of India in 1943. Since then, telecommunications in India has been a public utility owned by the Central Government with its operation and maintenance regulated by the Indian Telegraph Act of 1885 (ITA) and the Wireless Telegraphy Act of 1933.

At the time of independence, the government took charge of a network that connected only 82,000 subscribers in 321 exchanges. In the ensuing centralised planning process, resource allocation for the telecom sector was low and priority was given to sectors such as roads, power, sanitation, education, health etc. Till 1985, resource deployment in the telecom sector was around 2 to 3 per cent of the total budget allocation. With no access to any other sources of funds, this sector registered low to moderate growth.

At the beginning of the Seventh Five Year Plan in 1985, the Government decided to focus on improving this sector and constituted the Telecommunications Board and the Department of Telecommunications (DoT) within the Ministry of

Communications to oversee operations, maintenance and development of telecom services (telecom was till then under the purview of the Posts and Telegraph Department within thc Ministry of Communications). A new emphasis was also laid on the funding of the telecom sector. Whereas the plan budget of the Department of Telecom was still regulated by the central planning process and the Ministry of Finance, it was agreed in principle that additional resource mobilisation through market borrowing will be permitted in respect of the telecom sector.

The most striking success of liberalization policy is visible in telecommunications. Teledensity has risen dramatically, an entire industry with private players has come about, privatisation has begun with VSNL, and new technologies have come about. Looking forward, the telecom sector will feature lively competition between multiple private firms, with a strong role for TRAI to establish pro-competitive policies.

New Telecom Policy (NTP), 1999 provides the basic framework for the future development and growth of the telecom sector in the country. The NTP took into account the far-reaching technological developments taking place in the telecom sector globally and stressed on implementing the Governments' resolve to make India a global IT superpower. The objectives of the NTP are to

- Make available affordable and effective communications for the citizens.
- Strive to provide a balance between the provision of universal service to all uncovered areas, including the rural areas and the provision of high-level services capable of meeting the needs of the country's economy.
- Encourage the development of telecommunication facilities in remote, hilly and tribal areas of the country.
- Create a modern and efficient telecommunications infrastructure taking into account the convergence of IT, media, telecom and consumer electronics and thereby propel India into becoming an IT superpower.
- Convert Public Call Offices (PCOs), wherever justified,

into Public Teleinfo Centres offering multimedia services like Integrated Services Digital Network (ISDN) services, remote database access, government and community information system etc.

- Transform in a time bound manner, the telecommunications sector to a greater competitive environment in both urban and rural areas providing equal opportunities and level playing field for all players.
- Strengthen research and development (R&D) efforts in the country and provide an impetus to build world-class manufacturing capabilities.
- Protect the defence and security interests of the country.
- Enable Indian telecom companies to become truly global players.

Under NTP, the government no longer engages in telecom service provision, which is now the task of private and public sector companies operating in a competitive market. The Telecom Regulatory Authority of India (TRAI) now performs the regulatory functions of the sector. The Department of Telecom and the Telecom Commission have re-focused on the functions of policy formulation, licensing, wireless spectrum management, administrative monitoring of PSUs, research and development and standardization/validation of equipment etc. Some major initiatives in telecom policy in recent years have included the following.

- Opening up of international long distance tariff.
- Permitting internet telephony.
- Setting up a mechanism for Universal Social Obligation (USO).
- Permitting a fourth operator in the cellular mobile segment.
- Commissioning of National Internet Backbone (NIB).

The NTP, 1999 has envisaged that India should emerge as a major manufacturing base and major exporter of telecom equipment. The manufacturing capacity of the indigenous industry is small in relation to the other major operators in the world and exports constitute a very small proportion of the total production of telecom equipment in the country. Promoting exports as a thrust area and development of India multinationals should be among the major goals in this sector. To achieve this objective, the Tenth Plan aims at removing the various constraints relating to transfer of the latest technology, access to cheap international finance, joint ventures with foreign companies, rationalization of custom and import duties on inputs and development of a strong industry-sponsored R&D base. Due to fast changing technology in this sector and the existing technological gap in relation to the developed countries, India will have to rely on transfer of technology in a big way in the immediate future. To achieve this, strategic alliance with leading international companies will have to be an integral part of the overall exercise of technology transfer.

8.2.1 Bharat Sanchar Nigam Limited (BSNL) and Mahanagar Telephone Nigam Limited (MTNL): The telecommunications network of these two public sector undertakings is one of the largest telecom network in Asia. BSNL provides a cost-effective alternative to mobile subscribers with low entry charges, no security deposit for local/ISD connection, no CLIP charges, no additional airtime charges while roaming in BSNL network, free zonal roaming for pre-paid subscribers, no monthly charges for national roaming under Plan 325, free SMS services for both incoming and outgoing to all prepaid customers and additional grace-period of 90 days for SIM-activation without activation charges.

In order to supplement the efforts of public sector providers and to ensure greater competition in providing basic telephone services, private companies are being licensed to offer basic services.

MTNL, the telecom operating company for the cities of Delhi and Mumbai was created in 1986. It was decided that MTNL be authorised to raise funds as a frontal agency for the DoT. The growth of the telecom sector underwent a qualitative change after resource mobilisation was allowed through

MTNL.

8.2.2 Telecommunications Regulatory Authority of India (TRAI): TRAI has taken the following measures in recent years with a view to obtain a sound framework for competition between multiple technologies and vendors.

TRAI has given two recommendations on VSAT. First relates to issuance of licenses for VSAT services such as 'Receive only VSAT' because it has great potential to open new vistas of innovation in information sharing and spread of education and in facilitating the efforts of the government in bridging the Digital Divide. The second recommendation relates to facilitating VSAT operations by permitting Higher Data Rate, Reduction in Licence fee for Captive VSAT Network and reducing minimum antennae size. In order to promote internet in the country, TRAI has made a number of recommendations including setting up of National Internet Exchange of India (NIXI). In order to ensure for the consumers equal ease of access to different domestic and international long distance service providers, TRAI has issued a directive to all access providers and national/ international long distance operators regarding implementation of carrier selection in their respective network. A regulatory principle was maintained to prevent any anti-competitive or predatory behaviour on part of dominant operators.

The quality of services of all service providers is being monitored by TRAI on the basis of quarterly reports submitted by them. TRAI is also conducting an objective survey of Quality of Service (QoS) parameters of basic and cellular service in different circles through an independent agency. The agency has also been assigned the task of making an assessment of customer satisfaction through a survey. TRAI has also issued a regulation on quality of service for Voice over Internet Protocol (VOIP) based International Long Distance Service.

It has recommended deregulating regulatory intervention

in cellular tariffs. This implies that operators no longer need to have prior approval of the regulator for implementing tariff plans except under certain conditions. Guidelines were also issued to service providers in respect of pre-paid cards which would enable increased consumer awareness and transparency for the subscriber.

It has finalized the System of Accounting Separation, providing a detailed accounting and financial system maintained by telecom service providers and has forwarded the same to DoT for notification under Section 35(2)(d) of the TRAI Act. The proposed system, based on the principles of accounting separation, would help monitor and measure financial performance of individual telecom products/ network services and help disinvestment aggregate costs to the level of network elements. It would also help in identification of cross-subsidisation practices in the industry, wherever these exist. By providing for maintenance of detailed cost records right up to the level of network elements, the system will help generate accurate information on costs, which is necessary for tariff and interconnected regulations. TRAI's document on accounting separation would go a long way in promoting healthy competition with adequate mechanisms built in to detect unfair competitive practices. While the system is mainly aimed at enabling better monitoring and control by TRAI, the new system is also expected to help operators establish a more comprehensive system for arriving at product/network service wise costs and revenues and thus enhance their operating efficiency.

The National and International Long Distance markets in telecom have been opened up to competition. These policy measures have resulted in significant reduction in long distance tariffs due to competitive pressures. This has drastically reduced the margin available to fund the Access Deficit incurred. In a multiple operator environment, it is important to specify an International Usage Charge (IUC) regime which gives greater certainty to the Inter-operator settlements and facilitates inter-connection agreements. Therefore, TRAI notified its Telecommunication Inter-connection Usage Charges (IUC) Regulation, 2003 in January 2003 which covered arrangements among service providers for payment of Inter-connection Usage Charges for telecommunication services, covering basic services which include WLL (M) service, Cellular Mobile Service providers and Long Distance Operators throughout the territory of India. This regulation has specified the IUC for origination, transit and termination in a multi-operator environment.

8.3 Vision for the Future

According to Economic Survey, 2006-07, "By the end of 2012, a total of 650 million telephone connections (including 66 million wired and 584 million wireless connections) are expected to be achieved. Concurrently, there is also a vision of providing 200 million rural telephone connections, which translates into a rural tele-density of 25 per cent. Broadband connectivity would be made available on demand, without limiting the speed. Each village would have at least one broad-band enabled kiosk. Broad-band connection would be provided to schools, health centres and panchayat offices. It is also envisaged that internet and broad-band subscribers will increase to 40 million and 20 million, respectively, by 2010." [1]

India is the preferred location for software vendors for its quality and cost. India has strong Unix base which provides opportunity for the development of products for internet based applications. Further, India has global connectivity with international dialling facility from over 13220 locations, leased/switched high-speed data links from major centres through STPs and VSNL. Internet connectivity is provided through several networks. Abundant investment opportunities exist in the following thrust areas in India:

- Communication Infrastructure.
- Optic Fibre Cable.

- Gateways.
- Satellite-based Communication Wireless.
- Software Development.
- IT-enabled Services.
- IT-education.
- IT-enabled education.
- Data Centres and Server Farms.

The future policies and programmes for the telecom sector should be guided by the basic goal of creating a world-class telecom infrastructure in order to meet the requirements of IT based sector and needs of a modernizing economy on the least cost basis. Ensuring value for money to the consumers and easy and affordable access to basic telecom services to every one and every where, should be the other goal of policies. The major objectives for the future should include the following.

- Affordable and effective communication facilities to all citizens.
- Provision of universal service to all uncovered areas, including rural areas.
- Building a modern and efficient telecommunications infrastructure to meet the convergence of telecom, IT and the media.
- Transformation of the telecommunications sector to a greater competitive environment, providing equal opportunities and level playing field for all the players.
- Strengthening R&D efforts in the country.
- Achieving efficiency and transparency in spectrum management.
- Protecting the defence and security interests of the country.
- Enabling Indian telecom companies to become truly global players.

Note

1. Government of India, Economic Survey, 2006-07, p. 190.

9

Tourism

9.1 Introduction

Tourism enhances the quality of life, preserves the national heritage and encourages the appreciation of diverse cultures both by domestic and foreign visitors. It has become an important segment of Indian economy as it generates employment opportunities and contributes substantially to its foreign exchange earnings.

Tourism industry is a composite of service providers such as travel agents, tour operators, transport operators, guides, hoteliers, guesthouse owners, entertainment organizers, shop owners, government departments, immigration and customs services, trainers and academicians. The industry benefits the economy in several ways such as generation of income, expansion of employment opportunities, mobilization of foreign exchange, social integration, cultural transformation and development of commerce.

A recent report of the World Travel and Tourism Council (WTTC) reveals that tourism and travel industry of India contributes substantially every year to the GDP and provides 17.4 million jobs. The Report has envisaged that the over all economic activity stimulated by the industry would grow at the annual rate of about 8.4 per cent over the next decade. This growth would result in the industry accounting for more than one in 15 jobs and contributing about 6.9 per cent to GDP by the end of 2010 AD. The Ministry of Tourism, Government of India, functions as the nodal agency for the development of tourism within the country and for attracting foreign tourists. It has now come out with a National Tourism Policy which pledges, inter alia, to make tourism and travel an important instrument for sustainable human development, poverty alleviation, and employment generation. Contribution of travel and tourism in GDP and employment is shown in Table 9.1.

Table 9.1: Contribution of Travel and Tourism (T&T) in GDP and Employment in 2007

	India (%) 2007	World average % during 2007	World average % Estimated in 2017
Contribution of T&T Economy to GDP	5.4	10.4	10.7
Contribution of T&T Industry to GDP	2.0	3.6	3.4
Contribution of T&T Economy employment	5.5	8.3	8.3
Contribution of T&T Industry Employment	2.3	2.7	2.8

Source: Government of India, Planning Commission, *Eleventh Five Year Plan* (2007-12), Volume III, p. 245.

In developed countries, the academia-industry link has resulted in cross-fertilization of ideas and this has yielded benefits for both. In the present day set up of India, we have too much information and too little knowledge. Information is to be converted into knowledge through a systematic process. Knowledge to tourism industry can be generated only through the interaction between academia, professionals, industrialists and government. As the national knowledge assets and organizational innovations become the key factors in determining economic strength, tourism industry must learn, adapt and adopt for attaining growth and development. Table 9.2 reveals India's share in world earnings from tourism.

9.2 Tourism Products in India

Tourism in India has an impressive variety of tourism products: heritage and culture tourism (with the 26 and 14 potential World Heritage Sites at the core); eco-tourism (wild life in National Parks); adventure tourism (mountain climbing, mountain trekking, river-based sports including rafting, and skiing); wellness (ayurveda and yoga institutes in Kerala and Rishikesh) and medical tourism (being developed by private sector hospital chains); beach tourism (centred around Goa); religious tourism (Varanasi, Haridwar, Tirupati, Bodh Gaya, Ajmer, to name a very few); MICE (meetings, incentives, conferences and exhibitions) tourism; desert tourism; and finally rural tourism.

Table 9.2: Tourism Receipts

Year	World Earnings	Earnings by India	Share of India in World Earnings
2002	487.0	2.9	0.60
2003	533.1	3.5	0.66
2004	633.0	4.8	0.75
2005	678.0	5.7	0.85
2006	735.0	6.6	0.89

Source: Government of India, Planning Commission, *Eleventh Five Year Plan* (2007-12), Volume III, p. 246.

Undoubtedly tourism in India has a remarkable variety and contributes substantially to the economy, particularly in providing jobs, full time or part time. Growth in international tourist arrivals during recent years has been significant. International tourism has also provided sustenance to the Indian handicrafts industry (carpets and other handcrafted textile products; brassware; inlaid marble and rosewood; bidri; papier mache etc). However, the Revealed Comparative Advantage (RCA) of India in travel services has been on the decline.

Many Indian leisure travellers find it more attractive to travel to foreign destinations than to destinations within the country and a substantial proportion is travelling to countries in the region, most notably Malaysia, Thailand and Singapore. What are the impediments that lie at the root of this lack of competitiveness in tourism? Paucity of tourist accommodation, inadequate transportation arrangements made expensive by deficient infrastructure and taxation, inadequate development of tourist destinations, which are bereft of ambience and lacking in amenities for tourists and facilities for their entertainment are some of the major causes. One aspect that is becoming increasingly relevant is the sheer shortage of places of entertainment within a motorable distance of cities where families may go for leisure purposes for weekends. Most of the hill stations in both North and South India are highly overcrowded during the season and is avoided by the tourist class that has the a large disposable income. There are other more specific problems also and we take them all up in turn. Table 9.3 shows recent trends in arrival of tourists in India.

Table 9.3: Tourists Arrivals in India

(Million)

Year	World Tourist Arrivals	Foreign Tourist Arrivals (in India)	Domestic Tourist Visits	Share of India in World Arrivals (%)
2002	706.4	2.38	269.6	0.34
2003	693.2	2.73	309.0	0.39
2004	761.0	3.46	366.2	0.46
2005	802.0	3.92	390.5	0.49
2006	842.0	4.45	461.2	0.52

Source: Government of India, Planning Commission, *Eleventh Five Year Plan* (2007-12), Volume III, p. 246.

9.3 Beach Tourism

Beaches are one of the most important destinations for the affluent tourists from the Northern hemisphere. India has a coastline of 6000 kms but beach tourism is not well developed, Goa being the only international beach destination in the country. One factor, which affects the competitiveness of beach tourism in India, is the stringent coastal regulations zone requirements (CRZ), under which a hotel cannot be built within 200 metres of the coast. Such a restriction does not exist in any successful beach destination in the world. In 1992 the Ministry of Environment and Forests (MOEF) had issued orders for relaxation of the requirement so as to enable hotels to be built between 200 and 100 metres of the beach. The Hon'ble Supreme Court also issued a direction asking the Government to identify the stretches on the coastline on which beaches could be developed and report back to them. Although 15 years have elapsed this work has not been completed, as the MOEF has got involved in the task of comprehensive revision of the CRZ Regulations.

To improve India's competitiveness in beach tourism the Group recommends that a decision be taken quickly on hotel construction on beaches according to the prevailing practice in other countries. The sensitive areas could be clearly defined and one or two long stretches of the coastline, particularly on the west coast, could be opened up for development of tourism.

9.4 Conference Tourism

Meetings, incentives, conferences and exhibitions (MICE) is another area of tourism in which India lacks in competitiveness because of lack of world class conference centre apart from Delhi's Vigyan Bhawan, which is normally reserved for Government conferences. It is estimated that about 500 large annual conferences are held in India by domestic organisations alone. This has the potential to give India a competitive edge, as the conference centre would have assured business for a large number of days in the year. But what needs to be done is to facilitate the establishment of four or five large convention centres in the country. So far a large facility has been built in Hyderabad and another conference centre is proposed to be taken up in Dwarka in Delhi. In order to have more convention centres it would be necessary for the States to facilitate the allocation of land and for the Central

Government to give such centres infrastructure status under Section 80- 1A of the Income Tax Act, so that they can have tax benefits.

9.5 Entertainment for Tourists

Whether it is heritage tourism or beach tourism, the foreign tourists as well as domestic leisure travellers want some form of entertainment, particularly in the evening. For this purpose consideration needs to be given to allowing casinos to operate in certain locations. Though the subject has remained a taboo in the country it has to be borne in mind that casinos will not only increase the competitiveness of tourism destinations in the country but also have the potential to generate substantial revenues for the State Governments, just as lotteries have done for some of them. Casinos are the mainstay of the economies of tourist destinations such as Las Vegas, Monte Carlo and Macau. Singapore too has allowed the establishment of two casinos in its territory.

For heritage sites sound and light shows are a favourite form of entertainment. Such shows are being held by the State Tourism Departments in some tourist destinations but they are of poor quality. It is necessary to hold such shows at a larger number of major historical sites and substantially improve their quality.

9.6 Tourist Clusters

In the affluent countries there is flow of tourists out of the cities not only during holidays and almost every weekend, weather permitting. The weekend tourists, particularly those with children, normally go out short distances to resorts and tourist destinations, such as mountains, lakes and beaches. But they also go to man made attractions and clusters of attractions such as Santosa Island Resort in Singapore.

9.7 Maintenance of Heritage Sites

The Archaeological Survey of India (ASI) has the responsibility for the maintenance and upkeep of all monuments and archaeological sites notified by the Government of India as a protected monument under the Ancient Monuments and Archaeological Sites and Remains Act, 1958. Some of the States have also enacted similar legislation and notified monuments and archaeological sites under the Acts. The allocation of funds made available to the ASI is grossly inadequate for the maintenance and restoration of the monuments and the environs of these monuments. The difference that adequate funds can make to a monument has been well illustrated by the case of Humayun's Tomb in New Delhi, which has been transformed with the help of donations from the Agha Khan Foundation. Paucity of funds is also a contributory factor for the present state of neglect in which the Delhi Red Fort finds itself. The position is not very different in the case of monuments protected by the State Governments. In a large number of monuments not even minimum facilities such as provision of drinking water and toilets has been provided.

9.8 Infrastructure Development of Tourist Sites

Schemes for the development of infrastructure at tourist sites have been undertaken under the Five year Plans and some good results have been obtained. But the funds have been spread thinly and the schemes have not been integrated with plans for the beautification of the urban surroundings of the sites. Several cities with tourist interest have been included in the 63 cities identified as mission cities under the Jawaharlal Nehru Urban Renewal Mission (JNNURM), but the priority in the Mission is for schemes for water supply, sewerage, drainage and solid waste management. In order to improve the competitiveness of heritage tourism in India the Group recommends that funds should be earmarked from the provisions for JNNURM for the beautification of the urban surroundings of the heritage sites in these cities.

A large number of foreign and domestic tourists use dedicated tourist vehicles mainly buses for visiting tourist destinations and the private sector has made large investments in these vehicles. The road and passenger tax regimes of the State Governments increase the cost of travel but more importantly they are a source of harassment to the tourists because of the manner of their implementation. Some States charge taxes on a quarterly basis, some per day and others on a per seat basis, which could be in addition to the quarterly charges. The buses carrying tourists have to stop at the borders for long periods every trip as the papers are checked and taxes collected where necessary. Even if the quarterly or daily taxes have been paid there is no respite from standing in the queue along with other such vehicles and trucks. The problem is exacerbated by the limited and over worked staff.

In order to save the tourist vehicle operators and the tourists from harassment the Group recommends that by an amendment in the Motor Vehicles Act the tourist buses may be given a distinct number plate. Taxes should be chargeable on a quarterly or six-monthly basis and it should be made possible for the buses to enter a State just by swiping a smart card showing that taxes have been paid. In order to make this workable swiping facilities should be provided at all points on inter state borders. The Group is also of the view that is strong case for abolishing per seat passenger tax on the same logic as most States have abolished octroi.

Road connectivity is crucial for the development of tourism. While the entire network of National Highways and State Highways has to be maintained in good condition for the development of the economy it is important that all current and proposed World Heritage sites and other tourist destinations are connected to airports and/railway stations with single/double/four-lane roads (depending on the traffic intensity) and maintained in good condition with adequate allocation of funds for repair and maintenance. A monitoring system should be created to ensure that the roads leading to important tourist destinations are kept in good condition. For this purpose associations of tourist bus operators could be asked to post information on the website of the Ministry of Tourism about any deterioration in the condition of National Highways of tourist interest and on the websites of the State Departments of Tourism about the State Highways. On the basis of information received on the website the Ministry of Tourism for National Highways and the State Tourism Department for State Highways should take up the question of repairs and maintenance or even upgradation of the roads with the agencies/authorities concerned (NHAI or State PWD).

9.9 Human Resource Development

As in some other service sectors there is a large skill deficit in the tourism sector, which is impeding its development and impinging on its competitiveness. There are 26 Institutes of Hotel Management (IHMs), which have come up with Central financial assistance, and 12 more are in the pipeline. There are 125 private institutes affiliated to various universities/boards, which run hotel management courses. There are 6 Food Craft Institutes (FCIs) run by the Central Government and four more have been sanctioned and 20 run privately. The hotel management institutes including the private ones are producing 14000 graduates annually and the FCIs 4000 workers in the skilled categories. It is estimated that there is 35% attrition to other industry leaving only about 9000 graduates and 2500 skilled workers available annually to the hotel industry. Against this the annual requirement is estimated at 69,000 in managerial and 1.34 lakh in skill level categories. Thus there is a very large shortage of skilled personnel in the hospitality sector and the deficit is more acute in non-managerial categories.

The hotel management courses (of four years) fall under the purview of the All India Council of Technical Education (AICTE), but by virtue of a dispensation granted by the Hon'ble High Court the National Council of Hotel Management & Catering Technology (NCHMCT) has been performing the regulatory functions, fixing the curriculum and affiliating hotel management institutes, holding examinations and granting degrees to graduates in the tie up with the IGNOU. The NCHMCT has also undertaken the regulatory work in respect of the food craft institutions, although a large majority of private institutions remain unrecognised and are not seeking affiliation.

The Indian Institute of Travel & Tourism Management (IITM) is an institute affiliated to the All India Council for Technical Education, running courses for tour operators and holding examinations and granting diploma. The IITTM also conducts short-term courses for tour guides, holds examinations and grants diplomas for the profession.

The Ministry of Tourism is proposing to set up 9 more IHMs and 25 more FCIs, so that each State has one IHM (with some tourist oriented States having two) and one FCI. Initiatives are also proposed to make the Industrial Training Institutes, Polytechnics and Secondary Schools in the vocational streams to undertake programmes for increasing the supply of personnel in the skill categories. In the Group there was full support for all these initiatives but the Group also felt that even after all of them fructify there will still remain a huge shortage of skills in the hospitality sector.

Since IHMs can be run on a self-sustaining basis, the only help that privately run IHMs may need is allocation of land at reasonable cost or on long term lease by the State Governments. The requirement of hospitality personnel in the skilled categories is however very large and much wider initiative for undertaking vocational training programmes is required than is being envisaged at present.

10

Taxation of Services in India

10.1 Introduction

Service sector is very wide in its range. It includes, inter alia, health care, education, social security, leasing, entertainment, credit rating agencies, telecommunications, transport, publicity and advertising, insurance, banking, legal and financial services.

From equity point of view, services should be taxed in the same way as goods. Taxation of goods and exclusion of services distorts the relative prices of goods vis-à-vis services, encouraging artificially the demand for services. In the process, the allocation of resources is also distorted. If tax is imposed on goods and not on services, a relatively high rate of tax would be required on goods to generate a given amount of revenue. If tax is imposed both on goods and services, a moderate tax rate can yield the given revenue. Administratively, taxation of both goods and services is desirable because it would reduce disputes pertaining to distinction between goods and services.

Like goods, services can also be classified into two broad categories: essential services (e.g. health and education) and luxury services (e.g. entertainment and tourism). The rationale for exemption/lenient tax treatment of essential services is the same as for essential goods. Similarly, luxury services should be taxed at a high rate like luxury goods.

10.2 Constitutional Provisions

A scrutiny of List II (State List) in the Seventh Schedule of the Constitution of India shows that State Governments are empowered to tax entertainment and professional services (entries 16 and 18 of List II). The Central Government had no specific powers to tax services when it introduced service tax on select services in 1994. It was done under its residual powers of taxation vide entry 97 of List I (Union List in the Seventh Schedule). The collection of service tax was entrusted to the excise department.

However, the Constitution (Eighty-eighth Amendment) Act, 2003 put service tax in the Union List by inserting entry 92C in that List. Furthermore, service tax was put under Article 268A of the Constitution which specifies that the principles of collection and appropriation of taxes on services will be determined by Parliament. In other words, revenue from service tax is outside the purview of the Finance Commission.

The need to tax service sector is well recognised by the Government. To quote, "The tax revenue from the agricultural sector being negligible, the industrial sector continues to constitute the only principal tax base though it has suffered a reduction in the share of GDP over the period. Despite the fact that the services sector has shown substantial buoyancy, its contribution to the exchequer is not significant in relation to its sizeable share in GDP. Thus, in order to impart buoyancy to the revenue receipts and to provide consistency and equity in the tax structure via-a-via the composition of income, it is imperative to bring a major part of the services sector under the tax net." [1]

Although the contribution of service sector to GDP has increased over the years, the tax system has remained confined mainly to commodity production. In this connection, the Finance Minister observed in his 1994-95 budget speech, "There is no sound reason for exempting services from taxation when goods are taxed and many countries treat goods and services alike for tax purpose." [2] The Tax Reforms Committee (TRC) [Chairman: Raja Chelliah], 1991 also recommended imposition of tax on certain select services, viz. advertising, non-life insurance and telephone services and services of stock brokers.

10.3 Present Structure of Service Tax

In view of the need for additional resources, rising contribution of service sector to GDP and the recommendations of TRC, a modest effort was made in the 1994-95 budget when a 5 per cent tax was imposed on telephone and non-life insurance services and services of stock brokers with effect from July 1, 1994. The coverage of service tax was extended to advertising, courier and radio paging services from November 1, 1996.

In his 1997-98 budget speech, the Finance Minister maintained that services are products as much as manufactured goods and hence both must bear taxes. With these considerations in view he extended the service tax to the services provided by the following: transporters of goods by road, consulting engineers, custom house, steamer and clearing and forwarding agents, air travel agents, tour operators and car rental agencies, outdoor caterers, pandal contractors and mandap keepers, and manpower recruitment agencies.

In the 1998-99 budget, service tax on the transportation of goods by road, outdoor caterers, and pandal contractors was abolished. However, its net was extended to services provided by architects, interior decorators, management consultants, chartered accountants, cost accountants, company secretaries, private security services, real estate agents and real estate consultants, market research agencies, credit rating agencies, underwriting agencies, and slaughter houses using mechanised means for large animals.

Acknowledging the potential of service tax, the Finance Minister in his 2000-2001 budget speech announced the setting up of an Expert Group to go into all its aspects and make suitable recommendations. The net of service tax was greatly expanded when the following 15 services were added to the list of taxable services in the 2001-02 budget.

1. Specified banking and financial services.
2. Authorised service stations for servicing of vehicles including two wheelers.

3. Port services.
4. Broadcasting services.
5. Photographic services.
6. Convention services.
7. Sound recording services.
8. Scientific and technical consulting services.
9. Telex services.
10. Telegraph services.
11. Facsimile services.
12. Online information and data base retrieval services.
13. Video tape production services.
14. Services auxiliary to insurance.
15. Services provided to lease circuit line holders.

In his 2004-05 budget speech, the Finance Minister announced the inclusion of some more services under the service tax ambit. These were the following.

1. Business exhibition services.
2. Airport services.
3. Services provided by transport booking agents.
4. Transport of goods by air.
5. Survey and exploration services.
6. Opinion poll services.
7. Intellectual property services other than copyright.
8. Brokers of forward contracts.
9. Pandal and shamiana contractors.
10. Outdoor caterers.
11. Independent TV/radio programme producers.
12. Construction services in respect of commercial or industrial constructions.
13. Life insurance services to the extent of the risk premium.

In the 2005-06 Budget, the following 9 items were added to the list of taxable services.

1. Transport of goods through pipeline or other conduit.
2. Site preparation and clearance, excavation, earth moving and demolition services, other than those provided to agriculture, irrigation and watershed development.

3. Dredging services of rivers, ports, harbours, backwaters and estuaries.
4. Survey and map making other than by Government Departments.
5. Cleaning services other than in relation to agriculture, horticulture, animal husbandry or dairying.
6. Membership of clubs or associations.
7. Packaging services.
8. Mailing list compilation and mailing.
9. Construction of residential complexes having more than twelve residential units of apartments together with common areas and other appurtenances.

The 2005-06 Budget also expanded the scope of certain existing services in the following manner.

1. Commercial or industrial construction service to include renovation of such building or civil structure, post construction completion and finishing services for such building or civil structure, construction, repair, alteration, renovation or restoration of pipeline or conduits.
2. Erection, commissioning or installation services to include specified installation services.
3. Maintenance or repair services to include maintenance or management of immovable properties, maintenance or repair including reconditioning or restoration undertaken as part of any contract or agreement.
4. Broadcasting services to include charges recovered by broadcasting agencies from multi-system operator and provision of direct to home signals to the customers.
5. Sound recording to include recording of sound on any media and includes post-production services such as sound mixing or re-mixing.
6. Video-tape production to include recording of any programme, event or function on any media and includes post production services.
7. Taxable services provided by authorised service station to include reconditioning or restoration of motor-cars, two

wheeled and light motor vehicles.

8. Beauty parlour services to include all services provided by beauty parlours.
9. manpower recruitment service to include supply of manpower, temporary or otherwise.
10. franchisee service to cover all agreements by which, the franchisor grants representational rights to franchise to sell or manufacture goods or provide services identified with the franchisor.
11. business auxiliary service to include production or processing of goods for or on behalf of the client.
12. outdoor catering service to include catering from a place or premises provided, by way of tenancy or otherwise by the person receiving such services.

The Budget for 2006-07 added the following new services under the service tax net.

1. Service provided by a Registrar to an issue.
2. Service provided by Share Transfer Agent.
3. Automated Teller Machine operations, maintenance or management.
4. Service provided by recovery agent.
5. Sale of space or time for advertisement, other than in print media.
6. Sponsorship services provided to anybody, corporate or firm, other than sponsorship of sports events.
7. Transport of passengers, other than economy class passengers, embarking on international journey by air.
8. Transport of goods in containers by rail by any person, other than Government railway.
9. Business support services.
10. Auctioneers' service, other than auction of property under directions or orders of a court of law or auction by the Central Government.
11. Public relation service.
12. Ship management service.
13. Internet telephony service.

14. Transport of persons by cruise ship.
15. Credit card, debit card, charge card or other payment card related services.

In the 2007-08 Budget, service tax net was extended to the following services.

1. Services outsourced for mining of mineral, oil or gas;
2. Renting of immovable property for use in commerce or business; however, residential properties, vacant land used for agriculture and similar purposes, land for sports, entertainment and parking purposes, and immovable property for educational or religious purposes will be excluded;
3. Development and supply of content for use in telecom and advertising purposes;
4. Asset management services provided by individuals; and
5. Design services.

Keeping in view the social objectives of state policy, the Government of India has refrained from taxing services in the field of health and education. Table 10.1 records the growth in revenue from service tax in India.

10.4 Conclusion

The Indian tax system has traditionally relied on commodity taxation for generating revenue for the Central and State Governments. The two major commodity taxes of the Central Government are excise duties and customs duties while at the level of the States, sales tax is the main commodity tax, accounting for about two-thirds of States' own tax revenue.

The extension of excise duties to more and more commodities of the industrial/manufacturing sector has now reached a saturation point. However, the service sector remained outside the tax net till 1994. This pattern of tax structure development in India was contrary to the experience of most other countries where taxation of commodities and services grew hand in hand.

Table 10.1: Growth of Service Tax in India (Rs. crore)

Year	Number of services	Number of assesses	Tax rate (%)	Revenue (Rs. crore)
1994-95	3	3,943	5	407
1995-96	3	4,866	5	862
1996-97	6	13,982	5	1,059
1997-98	15	45,991	5	1,586
1998-99	26	1,07,479	5	1,957
1999-00	26	1,15,495	5	2,128
2000-01	26	1,22,326	5	2,613
2001-02	41	1,87,577	5	3,302
2002-03	52	2,32,048	5	4,122
2003-04	60	4,03,856	8	7,891
2004-05	75	7,40,267	10	14,200
2005-06	84	8,05,591	10	23,055
2006-07	99	---	12	38,169*
2007-08	104	---	12	50,200#

* Revised estimates; # Budget estimates.

Sources: Government of India, Economic Survey, 2006-07, p. 29, Table 2.4; Government of India, Budget Papers, Budget at a Glance, 2007-2008.

Presently, service tax is levied on as diverse services as credit rating on the one hand and mechanised slaughter houses on the other. It is clear that service sector in India constitutes a tax base with vast potential which has not been exploited as yet.

Notes

1. Reserve Bank of India, Report on Currency and Finance, 1998-99, p. V-6.
2. Government of India, Ministry of Finance, Budget Speech of the Finance Minister, 1994-95, Part B, p. 24.

Appendix

Edited Extracts from India's Eleventh Five Year Plan (2007-12) on Services Sector

CONSTRUCTION

Background: The development of physical infrastructure in the country and, consequently, the construction sector has been in focus during the last decade. The increasing significance of construction activities in the growth of the economy was also evident during the course of implementation of the Tenth Plan with areas like Transportation, Irrigation, Housing, Urban Development and Civil Aviation receiving greater importance. It is well established that the influence of the construction industry spans across several sub-sectors of the economy as well as infrastructure development, like industrial and mining infrastructure, highways, roads, ports, railways, airports, power systems, irrigation and agriculture systems, telecommunication systems, hospitals, schools, townships, offices, houses and other buildings, urban infrastructure including water supply, sewerage, drainage, etc., and rural infrastructure. Thus, it becomes the basic input for socio economic development.

Criticality to Economy: The contribution of construction to Gross Domestic Product (GDP) at factor cost in 2006-07 was Rs. 1,96,555 crore, registering an increase of 10.7% from the previous year. The share of construction in GDP has increased from 6.1% in 2002-03 to 6.9% in 2006-07. The increase in the share of construction sector in GDP has primarily been on account of increased Government spending on physical infrastructure in the last few years; with programmes like National Highway Development Programme and Pradhan Mantri Gram Sadak Yojana/Bharat Nirman receiving a major fillip of late. The construction industry is experiencing a great upsurge in the quantum of the work load, and has grown at the rate of over 10% annually during the last five years. Although various steps have been taken to strengthen the construction industry, it is crucial to take necessary measures in order to prepare the industry to meet the challenges of growth.

The importance of construction activity in infrastructure, housing and other asset building activities can be seen from the fact that the component of construction comprises nearly 60-80% of project cost of certain infrastructure projects like roads, housing etc. In projects like power plants, industrial plants, etc. the share is lower but remains critical. In terms of magnitude, construction activity is second only to agriculture. The construction industry also has major linkages with the building material manufacturing industry including cement/steel, bricks/tiles, sand/aggregates, fixtures/fittings, paints and chemicals, construction equipment, petrol/other petro-products, timber, mineral products, aluminum, glass and plastics. Construction materials account for nearly two-third of average construction costs. Based on an analysis of forward and backward linkages of construction, the multiplier effect for construction on the economy is estimated to be significant.

Employment in the Construction Industry: With around 27,770 enterprises involved directly in the activity of construction in 2005, the industry is one of the largest employers in the country and is characterized by a mix of both organized and unorganized entities. The employment figures have shown a steady rise from 14.6 million in 1995 to more than double in 2005 i.e. 31.46 million personnel comprising engineers, technicians, foremen, clerical staff, skilled and unskilled workers. Larger investments in infrastructure have resulted in increased demand for construction and, consequently, for construction engineers and technicians. However, due to the limited availability of engineers and technicians in general and the greater demand in sectors like

IT, there is a substantial drop in the percentage of qualified Engineers employed at work sites from 4.71% in 1995 to 2.65% in 2005, and similarly at Sub-Engineering levels from 2.46% in 1995 to 1.85% in 2005.

The strength of skilled work force has also been consistently and substantially going down from 15.34% in 1995 to 10.57% in 2005 whereas relative proportions of unskilled workers have gone up from 73.08% in 1995 to 82.45% in 2005. The workers community accounted for 93% of the total employment in the construction sector in 2005, with a predominance of migrant labour workforce. It is important to create a reliable information system for labour migration both at the destination as well as at the point of origin of migration to reduce vulnerability. As macro level data is often inadequate to capture the flow and pattern of migration, State centric surveys are required to fill in this gap. With several ambitious projects on anvil during the 11th Plan, the demand for construction manpower is going to grow at a consistent pace of at least 8 to 9 percent, thereby resulting in an annual accretion of around 25 lakh persons to the existing stock.

Developments during the Tenth Plan: During 2002-07, many milestones were achieved by the Indian construction industry in the areas of institutional finance, human resource development, dispute resolution, procurement procedures, safety and quality in the construction industry and disaster mitigation initiatives. The construction industry was accorded Industrial Concern Status under the IDBI Act, thereby providing the much needed impetus in terms of availability of finance to the construction industry. Many national initiatives in human resource management were implemented for the non-formal construction sector, addressing workers as well as engineers and management professionals in the industry. Other major initiatives included, inter-alia, the establishment of Arbitral Institutions for dispute resolution, development of institutions for safety and quality aspects, setting up of disaster mitigation and retrofitting clinics along with the training of professionals in disaster mitigation, improvement in procurement practices in public sector and development of regulatory manuals for procurement procedures, as well as dissemination of information regarding good practices and development of action framework for quality and safety audits, certification and training of manpower.

Strategies for the Eleventh Plan: The major challenge that the construction industry faces during the Eleventh Plan is to raise its delivery capabilities commensurate with the Plan targets for sectors like Transportation, Housing and Urban Development. The planned development of infrastructure would face constraints, unless the construction industry improves the delivery potentials by addressing crucial issues and impediments by bringing in systemic changes. The major issues in the construction industry have been detailed in the following sections.

Productivity in the Construction Industry: Since capacity building for the construction industry to achieve expected delivery capabilities is the key focus area, introduction of efficient technologies and modern management techniques to raise the productivity of the industry are vital. Research and development in the construction industry should be seen as a continuing activity, as the scientific and technological advancements are needed to strengthen and raise the technological base of the construction industry. Recognizing this, support to the national institutions engaged in scientific research as also incentives for private sector players to undertake in-house R&D needs to be provided.

The low technological level of the Indian construction leads to low value addition, productivity, quality and high time and cost overruns. A National Strategy and policy framework focusing particularly on productivity enhancement and cost reduction are required to be developed to match the envisaged work load and delivery targets. Introduction of new technologies, construction systems and energy efficient materials (preferably based on waste recycling) need to be adequately emphasized in the national strategy. For rural roads sector, there is a need for developing and introducing use of "marginal materials" to enhance cost effectiveness of works. Adequate funds should be earmarked in the field of research and development for identification of appropriate and alternate materials to reduce the cost of construction.

Management of information in contemporary construction projects is one of the biggest challenges that face project teams in the upgradation of productivity levels. Information technology can be leveraged to address issues related to tendering, bidding, bid evaluation, grading of construction entities, project execution logistics, project management, as well as financial accounting and reporting for the construction industry. An appropriate Management Information System should be developed and implemented at the national, district and local levels. Further, an institution needs to be nominated as the repository of National Data Base for Construction Industry.

Human Resource and Entrepreneurial Development Framework: The major impediments faced by the construction industry in raising the levels of productivity are the acute shortage of skilled manpower, both at worker and supervisory levels, as well as the lack of experienced construction engineers. The construction industry, particularly the highway and road construction sectors are facing acute shortages of contracting agencies. The present situation is marked by lack of a harmonized skill upgradation and certification programme for construction workers and lack of incentives and regulatory framework to prescribe a certain percentage of trained and certified manpower by contractors. There is also a need to encourage adequate intake of civil engineers in engineering institutions to mitigate the existing shortage.

One of the initiatives undertaken by Construction Industry Development Council (CIDC) is the training, testing and certification programme of construction workers. This initiative has resulted in successfully upgrading the skills of construction workers in 47 designated trades through training, testing and certification of the construction workers.

A National Plan for training and certification of construction personnel at all levels needs to be developed and implemented. The plan should include initiating a system of 'Graded Certification' depending upon levels of proficiency achieved. In order to meet the shortage of trained manpower, short terms courses in certain important trades may be introduced. The role of advisory and consultancy services in strengthening the stature of Construction Industry is vital. However, presently these services are only a small part of the overall construction services and need to be suitably upgraded.

Need to Reduce Construction Cost: It is estimated that the total cost of procuring, monitoring and supervising and other indirect costs of construction projects consists of about 22% of the cost of the asset that is created. The reduction of these and other transaction related costs would be decisive in improving the profitability of the Indian construction industry. Apart from the measures to improve productivity, as discussed in the earlier sections, efforts are also required to streamline procedures and mechanisms within the industry as well as enhance the levels of quality for the sector as a whole.

Contract Procedures: The present contract conditions, procedures of procurement of projects and services being used by various Project Authorities in the country, both in the public and private sector, need to be reviewed and harmonized. According to some estimates, the cost of procuring comprises 16% of the total construction cost for certain projects. Development of standard contract procedure, documents and evaluation criteria would lead to significant reduction in transaction cost and time. In order to enable fair competition as well as maintain the quality of output, the system of pre-qualification should be adopted for large PPP projects, whereby only those companies that meet the stringent qualification criteria would be short-listed and invited to make a bid. For smaller projects, especially those involving repair and maintenance, prequalification should be done periodically and bidding should be made on the basis of limited circulation. The guidelines issued by the Ministry of Statistics and Programme implementation in the form of a set of Uniform Contract Conditions, may be taken as a basis for further consultation with experts and stakeholders with a view to formulating standard contract and bidding documents. A shift from the current practices towards electronic tendering process, online publishing of tender notices, online contract bidding documents and reverse bidding would eliminate unfair competition and make the bidding process transparent.

Dispute Resolution: In the absence of institutionalized procedures and practices, arbitration continues to be costly and time consuming. As per a survey conducted in 2001 by the Construction Industry Development Council (CIDC), the amount of capital blocked in construction sector disputes was over Rs. 54,000 crore. To minimize disputes leading to time and cost overruns, proper project planning process should be encouraged and DPRs may be completed before technical sanction. After the Arbitration and Conciliation Act 1996 came into force, there has been an improvement in the number of disputes resolved. However, certain shortcomings remain to be addressed in the ad-hoc Arbitration process in terms of defined selection procedures and working ethics of Arbitrators, absence of specific rules for agreement and provision of a neutral body to administer and supervise Arbitration. In view of these deficiencies, there is a need to introduce new measures to resolve disputes in a fair, speedy, transparent and cost effective manner.

A procedure involving the amicable resolution by conciliation, failing which reference to arbitration by a Board of Arbitrators in accordance with the Rules of Arbitration of the International Center for Alternate Dispute Resolution, New Delhi should be followed. Moreover, institutional arbitration rules, panel of accredited arbitrators based on selection criteria to maintain quality, standards and code of ethics/conduct, norms for negotiable terms of appointment, management of arbitrator's fees, and monitoring and supervision of progress of case, etc. should be developed and institutionalized in line with Indian Arbitration and Conciliation Act 1996, after consultation with experts and stakeholders.

Quality and Standards: To make the Indian construction industry more competitive, aspects related to enhanced quality in construction products should be accorded attention at all levels. The inadequate quality in construction works emanates from lack of incentives for inducting new technology, lack of pre-qualification requirements for trained and certified workmen, lack of appreciation for life cycle costing approach and lack of adequate R&D. In order to enhance the technological capabilities of the industry, all stakeholders would be required to actively support training and certification levels for skilled workers, supervisors, managers and promote construction techniques (like Ready Mixed Concrete, pre-fab techniques), which use information technology.

The Performance Appraisal Certificate Scheme is being implemented for development and promotion of materials, products and systems under the joint initiatives of Building Materials and Technology Promotion Council (BMPTC), CIDC, Bureau of Indian Standards (BIS) and other agencies. Further, in view of the widespread infrastructural development programmes, covering both urban and rural areas, particularly for roads, highways and rural connectivity schemes, district level testing laboratories should be established for testing and quality evaluation of materials.

The importance and benefit of adhering to performance standards, both in inviting tenders and in implementation is being increasingly realized by construction entities and procurement agencies. BIS is formulating a performance standard for special jobs requiring high quality levels. Another development, aimed at enhancing quality in construction works, is that a large number of construction companies are working to obtain ISO 9000 series certification.

Construction Finance: The Indian construction industry is faced with high operation, maintenance and financial costs. This aspect is further exacerbated by inadequate access to institutional finance, especially for small contractors who execute over 90% of the total construction works. Moreover, subsequent to the conferring of Industrial Concern Status on the construction industry, existing financial institutions and banks should adopt construction industry-specific lending norms and eligibility criteria for the borrowers from the construction sector as well as introduce special incentives or schemes for financing import of hi-tech construction equipment for infrastructure projects.

Other Important Issues: Safety and Related Issues of Construction Workers: Workers employed in construction activity are highly vulnerable segments of labour force particularly because of its unorganized nature. The workers in construction industry are vulnerable to the inherent risk to the life and limbs. The construction activities are also characterized by poor training, temporary relationships between employer and employee, uncertain working hours, lack of basic amenities, inadequacy of welfare facilities and casual approach of employers towards the problems of workers. In the absence of adequate statutory provisions, the requisite information regarding the nature and number of accidents is also not generally available.

In the recent past, several initiatives have been taken for the improvement of the working conditions of the construction workers through the mandatory provision for instituting the Provident Fund scheme among casual workers and the introduction of the Workers Welfare Cess. The Building and other Construction Workers (Regulation of Employment and Conditions of Service) Act, 1996 was also enacted recognizing the need for a comprehensive Central legislation for regulating the safety, health, welfare and other conditions of service for construction workers. However, only a few States have implemented the provisions of the Act like the setting up welfare boards, and efforts need to be renewed to speed up the implementation of the Act.

Along with the provision of appropriate training facilities for safety aspects related to construction, vigilant Safety Management Teams adequately trained in compliance procedures and hazard and risk assessment, and documentation of inspections of stipulated measures for safety of workers are required to be put in place. As a substantial segment of the construction industry workforce, women workers need to be accorded special focus in terms of vocational training and skill upgradation as well as the provision of stipulated social benefits.

Asset Management and Maintenance: Although the construction of physical infrastructure has been receiving emphasis in successive Five year Plans, the maintenance of these assets that are created has not been accorded similar importance due to the absence of necessary framework, planning and professionals for asset maintenance. The present system of asset management needs to be reviewed and strengthened at the local, State and Central Government levels. A policy frame work for ensuring mandatory provision for maintenance of assets needs to be evolved.

Environmental Issues: Sustainable development concepts applied to the design, construction and operation of construction projects can enhance both the economic well-being and the environmental health of communities. Environmental Impact Assessment (EIA) is recognized as an important tool for integrating these objectives, wherein EIA should be a necessary pre-condition before construction projects beyond stipulated size are approved. Further, initiatives for ensuring adherence to international standards and regulations like the Environment Protection Act 2006 and the Energy Conservation Act of 2001 are also required. Various interdisciplinary organizations like CIDC and BMTPC have been set up to address the issues of environment friendly technologies and energy efficiency in building materials, along with Central and State Pollution Control Boards to approve, monitor and regulate projects from all sectors including construction keeping in view their impact on environment.

Construction Law: As per the prevailing scenario, any organization engaged in construction activity, requires registration under five different legislations, apart from obtaining licences under three enactments and being subject to inspection under twelve laws. Further, there are 27 statutes pertaining to labour only. The multiplicity of laws and authorities, anomalies in the existing legal systems and the complexities thereof, suggest the need for a Unified Construction Law along with the formulation of a single window arrangement. The Unified Construction Law should have chapters pertaining to national construction policy and plan; constitution and functions of Central and State construction authorities; dispute resolution and arbitration; grants, funds, accounts, audit and report; registration and other provisions.

Taxation: The construction sector experiences a very high incidence of direct and indirect taxes for construction and construction related activities, as compared to other sectors. The taxation and regulatory systems pertaining to construction should be reviewed with a view to rationalize the same and eliminate multi source taxation. Greater clarity needs to be brought out on the treatment of the sector as "Industry" or “Service” for taxation purposes.

Combating Natural Disasters: There is an increasing realization that the problem of natural disasters is grave because their frequency has recorded more than a five fold increase in the last two decades. Institutional arrangements are required to identify, prevent and mitigate the effects of natural disasters. New programmes need to be taken as per guidelines and programmes announced by the National Disaster Management Authority. The development of human resources and training of professionals in disaster mitigation, disaster resistant construction technologies and setting up of Retrofitting Clinics and Disaster Identification Centers in all major districts falling in disaster prone regions is also recommended.

Substantial national resources are being spent on building assets and the pace of investment is going to enhance considerably during the Eleventh Plan with several new projects related to transportation including rural roads, housing, industrial infrastructure, energy and agriculture slated for time bound implementation. Necessary modifications, amplifications and introduction of good practices need to be adopted to achieve the desired growth in the construction sector and to align it with global trends in terms of growth, quality and competitiveness.

Path Ahead

- Enhance capacity building in the construction sector by improving productivity through introduction of efficient technologies and modern management techniques.
- Reduce transactional costs through reviewing contract procedures and dispute resolution mechanisms.
- Enhance quality standards and provision of adequate institutional finance to the construction sector.
- Develop a National Plan for human resource development through training and certification of construction personnel.
- Accord greater importance to safety in construction activities by establishing trained and certified Safety Management Teams.
- Earmark funds in the field of research and development for identification of appropriate and alternate materials to reduce the cost of construction.

TOURISM

Overview: Tourism is a multi-sectoral activity characterized by multiple services provided by a range of suppliers. It is the largest service industry in the country. Its importance lies in being an instrument for economic development and employment generation, particularly in remote and backward areas. It is contributing towards overall socio economic improvement and accelerated growth in the economy. The economic benefits flow into the economy through growth of tourism in the shape of increased national and State revenues, business income, employment, wages and salary income. Tourism is overwhelmingly an industry of private sector providers and the public sector has a significant role to play in infrastructure areas either directly or through Public Private Partnership mode.

Tourism is one economic sector in India that has the potential to grow at a high rate and can ensure consequential development of the infrastructure of the destinations. It has the potential to stimulate other economic sectors through its backward and forward linkages and cross-sectoral synergies with sectors like agriculture, horticulture, handicrafts, transport, construction etc. The particular significance of tourism industry in India is its contribution to national integration and preservation of natural as well as cultural environments and enrichment of the social and cultural lives of people like preservation of monuments and heritage properties. This sector is also helping the traditional art forms, crafts and culture.

Global Status and Trends: Over the past few years, the Travel and Tourism industry has had to contend with a series of unprecedented challenges. International events, such as terrorism and SARS, and economic turbulence have led to significant changes in Travel and Tourism demand. At the same time, international events such as an increase in information and booking facilities made available over the Internet; an ongoing desire by consumers to travel more frequently; stronger branding and globalization by companies; and the expansion of low-cost carriers (LCCs) have acted as a catalyst, accelerating fundamental changes in market behaviour and travel patterns that have been slowly emerging over the past decade. While business plans have become increasingly short term, more and more Governments are starting to realize that they cannot leave the growth of travel and tourism to chance. This emerging global consciousness represents a great opportunity for this industry.

As per the estimates of World Travel and Tourism Council, the worldwide travel and tourism is expected to grow by 4.3 percent per annum between 2008-2017. The industry is expected to post US$ 7060.3 bn of economic activity (total demand) in 2007, which will increase to US$ 13,231.6 bn by 2017. The industry is expected to contribute 3.6 percent to Gross Domestic Product (GDP) in 2007 (US$ 1851.1 bn), which is expected to rise to US$ 3,121.7 bn in absolute terms but percentage wise it will decrease to 3.4 percent by 2017. The earnings from Travel & Tourism have made it one of the largest industries in the World and the fastest growing sector of global trade accounting for 10.4 percent of global gross domestic product, 12.2 percent of global exports, 8.3 percent global employment and 9.5 percent global capital investment.

India's Tourist Profile: Tourist growth in India has undergone a remarkable change during Tenth Plan. Foreign tourist arrival has increased by about 87 percent from a level of 2.38 million in 2002 to 4.45 million in 2006. Share of India in world tourist arrivals has increased from 0.34 percent to 0.52 percent during this period.

Similarly, the foreign exchange earnings have grown by about 147 percent during the same period (US$ 2923 million to US$ 6569 million), 0.9 percent of the international tourist receipts. The average per tourist earnings in India was about US$ 1476 against the world average of US$ 872 during 2006.

Domestic tourist visits has also grown rapidly during the Tenth Five Year plan from 269.6 million in 2002 to 461.2 million in 2006. According to the Tourism Satellite Account for India prepared by Ministry of Tourism, the contribution of tourism sector, including both direct and indirect to GDP and employment was 5.83 percent and 8.27 percent respectively during 2002-03. The corresponding share has been estimated to be 5.90 percent and 8.78 percent respectively

It is universally acknowledged that the tourism resources in the country have the potential to generate significantly higher levels of demand from the domestic and international markets, which if exploited intelligently in a sustainable manner, can prove to be the proverbial engine of growth for the economy.

Review of Tenth Five Year Plan: Against an outlay of Rs 2900 crore in the Tenth Five Year Plan (central sector) an expenditure of Rs 2635.67 crore (91 percent) has been incurred. In the Tenth Five Year plan period an emphasis was laid on positioning & maintaining tourism development as a national priority activity by enhancing and maintaining the competitiveness of India is a tourist destination and improving existing tourism products and expanding these to meet new market requirements by creating world class infrastructure developing sustained and effective market plans & programmes and giving special thrust to rural & small segment tourism. Through broad fields of development Ministry of Tourism focused on infrastructure development in five key destinations like Ajanta-Ellora, Bodhgaya, Rajgiri-Nalanda, Kurukshetra, Mahabalipuram etc. Information and technology was also given a major thrust to promote Indian Tourism products in the country and abroad. Human resource development and capacity building for service providers were given more importance. As a result more than 40,000 persons were given training through 24 Institutes of Hotel Management and 12 Food Craft Institutions. In addition to these, large re venue generating products like convention centers at Suraj Kund, Haryana luxury trains in Karnataka, night Safari Park at Jorepokhari in Darjeeling, West Bengal were developed through PPP mode.

Objective and Strategy for Eleventh Five Year Plan: Though the Working Group on Tourism for Eleventh Five

Year Plan has recommended a target of 10 million international tourist arrivals by 2011, the Vision Document presently being drafted by Ministry of Tourism envisages achievement of this target by 2010. As per this strategy, target for the year 2011 will be 10.25 million. This target is proposed to be achieved through diversification of principal source markets, improving the infrastructural facilities such as airports, roads, civic amenities at the tourist destinations, increasing the air seat capacity and connectivity, vigorous publicity, etc. For domestic tourism, the target to be achieved in 2010 and 2011 will be 725 million and 812 million respectively assuming an annual growth rate of about 12 percent over the level of 461 million domestic tourist visits in 2006.

In order to achieve international visitor levels of 10 million by the end of the Eleventh Five Year Plan, the emphasis would be on diversification of principal source markets to include countries such as South Africa, Israel, Spain, China, Japan, South Korea, Australia, Brazil, Argentina etc. which offer high growth potential and from where present level of inbound tourist is low. There is also a need to concentrate on countries like South Africa, Mauritius, Kenya, Malaysia, Fiji etc. with a large Indian Diasporas for higher tourist arrivals from those countries. Similarly, greater resonance needs to be created in NRIs and PIOs to visit the country of their origin and discover their roots. "Baby- Boomers" group in North America and Europe would be encouraged to visit India by creating in them the desire to discover one of the oldest civilizations of the world to enjoy the plurality of cultural enjoyment, offered by this country.

In order to meet the requirement of growth in traffic, there would be further creation of quality accommodation. It is estimated that 200,000 approved quality accommodation rooms would be required in 2011 against the current level of about 100,000 rooms. Domestic travel must complement international travel. This would help in optimizing the utilization of infrastructural facilities and also make the future investment viable. The possibility of constructing hotels on surplus land with Airport Authority of India near International Airports needs to be considered. The surplus Railway land at specified Railway stations may also be utilized for constructing budget hotels. The new forms of tourism like rural tourism, cultural tourism, adventure tourism, cruise tourism, MICE tourism and medical tourism need to be taken up with renewed zeal and efforts.

To achieve the above goals, suitable measures would be taken for:

- Positioning and maintaining tourism development as a national priority activity.
- Enhancing and maintaining the competitiveness of India as a tourist destination.
- Improving India's existing tourism products further and expanding these to meet new market requirements.
- Creation of world-class infrastructure.
- Developing strategies for sustained and effective marketing plans and programmes.
- Developing human resources and capacity building of service providers. Positioning and Maintaining Tourism as a national priority.

Effective linkages and close coordination among various Departments and Ministries of Government will be established to plan and implement a professionally managed and integrated communications strategy to increase awareness about tourism and its social and economic impact on the society. State Governments would be encouraged to set up land banks and streamline procedure and practices to facilitate investment in tourism sector. Enhancing and maintaining the competitiveness of India as a tourist destination.

Effective steps for easier and faster availability of visas, increasing air connectivity and seat capacity from overseas markets, improving facilities and quality of services at international and major domestic airports, rationalization of taxes and removing restrictions like RAP/PAP/ILP would facilitate tourist flow to the country.

Connectivity has been one of the impediments for the growth of tourism in India Steps taken during Tenth Five Year Plan to liberalize civil aviation sector to a large extent eased the position with regard to the availability of seats. While international airlines inducted more capacity, there is a growth in number of carriers providing domestic air services. The increase in capacity has not only resulted in meeting the demand of the air travel but also in lowering the airfares. The infrastructure facilities at the airports would be developed to meet the rising air traffic requirements. For the promotion of tourism in the country, trained personnel and workforce need to be provided at airports for increasing the quality of service at the airports. The possibility of extending facilities of visa on arrival would be considered for tourist originating from selected countries.

Quality of rail services would be improved to encourage tourists to travel by train. Budget hotels may be provided by railways in all metro cities within the realm of public-private partnership. Well maintained clean waiting rooms, basic amenities like drinking water, toilets, tea/coffee facilities, parking facilities for tourist vehicles may be available at railway stations.

All major tourist destinations/heritage sites should be well connected with the highways. Tourist's coaches have to queue up at the border for paying toll tax and transport tax at every barrier, which is harassment to tourists. The respective State Governments may introduce single toll collection point for free movement of tourist transport. Tourist transport vehicles may also be given separate identification under Motor Vehicles Act to allow free movement between States. Oil companies on the highways may be encouraged to provide basic amenities at petrol pumps.

India has a rich resource of both tangible cultural heritage in its monuments and sites and also an intangible cultural heritage in the form of its architecture, music, dance/drama, local rituals and traditions and other folk arts. Cultural and heritage tourism will be expanded to tap rich resources of cultural heritage in its monuments and sites. An integrated circuit linking heritage monument with culturally rich villages and towns around them are to be formed to enable and strengthen the development of cultural tourism in India. The National Highways Authority may consider facilitating provision of suitable tourism facilities on their routes such as budget tourist accommodation and improvements in wayside amenities on road side and highways. Beach and Coastal tourism on the beaches of Goa, Kerala and North Karnataka may be considered for development due to the easier accessibility of these places by air. Kerala and the Andaman & Nicobar Islands have already been developed as International cruise destinations.

Riverine tourism may be developed along traditional routes, which may have an exotic appeal as also help sustain villages and settlement along the routes. In this way, village tourism would also be promoted. Indian cuisine has caught the fancy of people across the globe. This can be capitalized by developing culinary tour routes into different regions for enthusiasts to taste and learn the authentic way. This will create highly skilled workforce of culinary professionals not only for India but also to promote Indian cuisine internationally. Wild life Sanctuaries and National Parks would also be made an integral part of the Indian tourism product. The tourism facilities at the parks may be enhanced and proper site and visitor management plans need to be prepared so as not to disturb the ecological balance and disturb the local habitat to have a sustained tourism product.

India offers the best Mountain based adventure tourism in the world in the Himalayas. Already a lot of work has been initiated in this segment but they have to be made comparable or better than what is being offered in the Alpine countries. India's medical expertise has been gaining popularity in the

West where the costs are prohibitive. The development of special interest tourism segment will accrue greater socio-economic benefits.

Indian textiles, handlooms and handicrafts its furniture and jewellery are already popular abroad. Now with Indian designers also receiving global recognition, shopping has become an integral part of a tourist's itinerary. Hence the development of dedicated shopping centers and the flow of special interest shopping tourist may be encouraged as it will help revive traditional crafts and craftsmen, textiles and weavers and give these families a livelihood.

Domestic tourism in India is mainly pilgrimage. Travel facilities as well as facilities at pilgrimage centers need to be strengthened and made more tourists friendly. Pilgrimage centers may be identified and integrated with new domestic tourist circuits where in transport, accommodation, catering and darshan are all synergized to make pilgrimage tourism into a popular and comfortable mode.

Creation of World-class Infrastructure: Quality infrastructure may be created for developing tourist products and for providing better services to both domestic and international tourists. Creation of tourism infrastructure has favorable impact on overall economic growth and employment and on the preservation of art, culture and heritage. Tourism projects like Destination Development are capital intensive, commercially un-viable and require financial support from Government. At the same time, it is necessary that such infrastructure is created with professional expertise of architects, landscaping experts and is then privately managed through a transparent process. Large revenue projects such as setting up of hotels, convention centers, golf courses, tourist trains, etc., normally have substantial gestation periods. These facilities may be created by private initiative with Government acting as a facilitator and catalyst.

Tourist sites and destinations need to be carefully selected on the basis of their potential to provide all infrastructure facilities required by the tourists within such destinations and circuits. Master Planning of destinations and circuits will be done by outstanding architects/consulting agencies with sensitivity towards conservation, preservation and aesthetics aspects to enable their development in an integrated holistic manner.

During the Eleventh Five Year Plan, the strategy for infrastructure development should be to select only 10 major Destinations and 6 Circuits on an annual basis. Destination Management needs attention and coordination at the 27 World Heritage Sites in the country, which are impacted by increasing number of visitors and are also subject to a number of regulatory authorities. For the development of rural tourism, a panel of professionals may be identified for selecting the rural sites, interacting with the community and preparing projects based on tourism potential of the site.

One of the major bottlenecks in creation of hotel infrastructure is non-availability of land for the purpose. The steps that may be taken are: (a) Master Plan of major cities should mark commercial sites for construction of hotels, convention and exhibitions centers; (b) the hotel sites should be allotted on long term lease basis or could be allotted under the PPP mode through joint venture, revenue sharing, etc.; (c) our endeavor should be that the hotels are allowed higher FAR/FSI so that more rooms and commercial spaces are created out of the same space and it also helps in generating sustainable revenues; (d)the land should also be allotted for building of Guest Houses in all major cities and tourist destinations, if possible (e) home stay programme under the Government of India Scheme of "Incredible India Bed & Breakfast" needs to be promoted by all State Governments by allowing such establishments to be treated as non-commercial.

Rural villages, which have immense cultural heritage potential, need to be developed to showcase India's vast heritage. Infrastructure and other tourist facilities should be developed and local community involved in the management so as to percolate tourism and its socioeconomic benefits to rural areas. The focus would be on both tangible heritage and intangible heritage. The tangible heritage represents the "hard" culture of a community, where as intangible heritage represents the "soft" culture – the people, traditions, folklore, music, dance, traditional games, mythology, rituals, customs, handicrafts, arts, festivals, events, storytellers, local markets, and also living human treasures.

Developing Strategies for Sustained and Effective Marketing Plans and Programmes: This objective can be achieved by evolving and maintaining a system of market research activities in India's major source markets to continuously receive, analyze and respond to information on pricing, security issues, health, safety and quality of tourism services and products, etc and make use of various technological tools, including the internet, for advertising for greater and wider impact. Besides, it is necessary to encourage e-commerce portals to extend effective marketing support to small and medium enterprises and also offer competitive packages.

Developing Human Resources and Capacity Building of Service Providers: Tourism sector in the country is witnessing a boom that may bring an exponential demand for work force at managerial, supervisory, skilled and semi-skill level. This increase in growth will have direct impact on the demand and supply mismatch that country is already passing through and trying to correct for providing of satisfactory service to visiting tourists. To bridge the widening gap at skill level, the existing Food Craft Institutes (FCIs) are required to be strengthened and new ones opened. To enlarge the scope, hospitality education need to be imparted through the network of Industrial Training Institutes (ITIs), Polytechnics and at + 2 stage as a vocational stream of the school system. Institutes of Hotel Management (IHMs), which are processing the bulk of manpower at managerial and skill level, need be strengthened and capacities augmented, with international linkages for quality and quantity output of human resources. New IHMs in the States/regions that have not been covered as yet should be established for proper distribution of Government resources. Through integrated efforts with States, IHMs under PPP should be encouraged. For the young untrained staff who continues to join the industry, the Government should through short term training programmes build capacities in order to provide quality service. A scheme is required to be mooted to examine and certify the large number of industry/conventional trained skill manpower available in the country. The existing scheme of 'Train the Trainer' should be strengthened and implemented countrywide for boosting availability of adequate trainers for training.

Capacity building of the service providers through shorter training courses should be taken up as an integral effort to strengthen/enlarge the manpower required by the hospitality industry. More Food Craft Institutes need to be opened to meet the demand for skilled personnel in food crafts. The training programmes must cover the skill development in general for fresh candidates, specialized skill development, including language courses, for fresh as well as existing service providers, basic skill up gradation in general for existing service providers, training of trainers programme and creating awareness of tourism benefits/knowledge in rural areas.

Promotion and Publicity: The Ministry of Tourism is carrying out its Promotion and Publicity in both overseas and domestic market vigorously. The strategy to be adopted for Eleventh Plan on publicity and marketing is to promote Indian tourism in the European markets like Italy, Spain, France, and Germany in the regional languages and in the Korean and Japanese markets in a focused manner. India should be promoted as a summer retreat in the months of July, August and September when many European & North American schools and colleges have their holiday breaks. The campaign should convey India as a "Year Round" Destination.2009 should be declared as "Visit India Year" as this will be very close to Common Wealth Games in 2010, and would enable a boost to inbound tourism. While producing Publicity material like brochures etc the key areas should be identified and a balance needs to be established between the print collaterals and the digital formats. While producing tourist literature, the availability of infrastructure and connectivity of the areas being marketed through the collaterals also needs to be taken into account.

Taxation, Incentives and Concessions: Provision of tax holiday to Travel & Tourism industry may be considered to encourage investments from non-tourism sector into tourism sector. The Ministry of Finance (Budget 2007-08) has accorded Tax holiday for 5 years for 2-star, 3-star and 4-star category of hotels in and in the adjoining district of Delhi for the Commonwealth Games. This needs to be extended if possible, throughout the country and for all categories of hotels. Special incentives may be considered for the hilly areas, rural areas and places of pilgrimage, North Eastern region including Sikkm, J&K, Uttaranchal and Himachal Pradesh. Each State Government has its own criteria for Luxury Tax varying from 5 percent to 20 percent. Rationalization of Luxury Tax and other tourism related taxes and levies may be considered by all the States. The Tax structure should not be based on announced tariff; rather it should be on the basis of actual payment made by the clients. There is acute shortage of hotel accommodation and in particular budget accommodation all over the country. Ministry of Tourism has estimated that there is a shortage of 1,50,000 hotel rooms all over the country. Out of this, 1,10,000 rooms are in the budget category. The subsidy/incentives should be on the room created basis and should be also applicable in metro towns and the procedure of disbursement of subsidy should be simple. In order to create standard budget accommodation, incentives may be given to Guest Houses and accommodation under the Home Stay programme of the Government also.

IT ENABLED SERVICES

Overview: Information Technology has marked a turning point in the history of global trade and services. With ever increasing availability of international bandwidth and powerful workflow management software, it is now possible to disaggregate any business process, execute the sub-processes in multiple locations around the world, and reassemble it, in near-real time, at another location. This is driving fundamental changes in the global IT services landscape. The vendors and customers are redefining the levels of value creation in the industry. IT also makes significant contribution in increasing productivity in various sectors of the economy. Indeed, the phenomenal growth of the Indian IT Software and Services and ITES-BPO sector has had a perceptible multiplier effect on the Indian economy as a whole. In addition to the direct positive impact on the National Income and employment generation, it has triggered a rise in direct-tax collections and propelled an increase in consumer spending, thanks to the significantly higher disposable incomes. Today, India has found its niche in the IT world and is regarded as the premier destination for the global sourcing of IT and IT-Enabled Services (ITES). The IT enabled services like Medical Transcription, Call Centers, Data Processing, Back-Office Operations, GIS, Revenue Accounting etc. are considered as niche areas of the country and the IT industry is now getting involved in providing end to end business solutions, system integration, remote management etc.

Review of Tenth Plan: The IT and IT-Enabled Services fall into two segments: (i) Exports and (ii) Domestic as described below.

IT Enabled Services (Exports Segment): India's success in the export of IT Software and Related Services over the past decade remains unparalleled. Total export revenues earned by this sector have grown from US$ 7.7 billion in 2001-02 to US$ 31.3 billion in 2006-07, thus showing a near 32% compound growth rate. India now accounts for 65 per cent of the global market in offshore IT and 46 per cent of the ITES market. A majority of the Fortune 500 and Global 2000 corporations are sourcing IT and ITES from India. While the US and the UK remain the dominant markets, contributing to 67 percent and 15 percent of total exports respectively, Indian firms are also keenly exploring new geographies for business development, and to strengthen their global delivery footprint.

Since the inception of IT industry in India, the companies have been focusing on quality initiatives, to align themselves with international standards. Over the years, the industry has built robust processes and procedures to offer world class IT software and technology related services. Today, India-based centers (both Indian firms as well as MNC-owned captives) constitute the largest number of quality certifications achieved by any single country. As of December 2006, over 440 Indian companies had acquired quality certifications with 90 companies certified at SEI CMM Level 5 – higher than any other country in the world.

The growth of the sector has led to tremendous payoffs in terms of wealth creation and generation of high quality employment. Market capitalization values of leading Indian IT companies now exceed those of global competitors, and the exports segment of the Indian IT-ITES sector directly employed over 920,000 people in 2005-06.

With only 10 percent of the US$ 300 billion market potential accessed so far, there is significant headroom for growth. Further, with the global off shoring market continuing to grow rapidly, as the proven benefits of off shoring (also termed global sourcing or global delivery) induce more and more companies to adopt these practices and providers develop the capabilities to offer more sophisticated products and services – the size of the overall pie is also expanding.

Key service lines and vertical markets including newly emerging sectors for the ITES industry are listed below:

Service Lines

1. R&D and engineering services

2. Consulting services
3. System integration
4. Application development and maintenance
5. Traditional IT outsourcing
6. Horizontal services (finance accounting and administration, customer interaction services, human resource administration, research, etc.)

Verticals (including newly emerging sectors)

1. Agriculture
2. Banking
3. Insurance
4. Manufacturing
5. Health Care and Pharmaceuticals
6. Travel and hospitality
7. Animation, media and entertainment
8. Biotechnology and life sciences
9. Nanotechnology
10. Courts and legal
11. Power and Energy
12. VLSI and CAD
13. Automobile and Transportation
14. Smart Governance

This represents a 'make or break' opportunity, capable of catapulting India into a high growth orbit and on a fast track to becoming a developed nation. Given that we are closely chased by other aspiring countries to grab a share of this pie, there has to be a concerted effort by the government and industry to maintain the lead position thus created and expand it further. The benefits of global leadership in these knowledge industries go far beyond the economic dimensions. As major global companies offshore more mission-critical work to India, their dependence on India increases thus providing significant strategic advantage. Domestic ITES-BPO segment The Banking and Financial Services, Communications and Media, Manufacturing (Consumer Durables/Automobile), Aviation, Hospitality, and Retail are some of the key verticals that primarily benefit from the ITESBPO services in the domestic market in India.

While cost savings have been the primary driver of offshore outsourcing, vendors do not have comparable differences in labour costs to leverage while serving the domestic market. As a result, the primary motivation for the domestic market, in its early years of evolution are not cost savings but access to specialist skills and freeing client resources to focus on the core business. Scalability and process efficiency are expected to result in some degree of cost savings in the domestic market as well. Notwithstanding its relatively smaller contribution to the industry revenues, this segment is witnessing a noticeable increase in interest and activity on the part of customer organizations as well as service providers. However, the total size of the domestic market is expected to cross US$ 8.335 billion in FY 2006-07, a growth of 28 percent over FY 2005-06. Although this segment has been led by MNCs in the past few years, Indian firms are gradually gaining ground. Over time, this segment would provide significant space for larger SMEs, as the mid-sized firms increase their levels of IT adoption.

Vision and Strategy for the Eleventh Plan

Vision: Our vision is to make India the most preferred destination for providing IT and ITenabled services (ITES) and creating the required eco-system to demonstrate the full potentials of the Indian skills and enterprise in this vital sector. The objective during the Eleventh Plan would be to make an effective and maximal utilization of ICT to improve the quality of life of the common man and promote inclusive growth, increase productivity and competitiveness and generate wealth and strength so that India emerges as a knowledge superpower in the comity of developed nations.

Strategy: India's performance in IT enabled and other high end services is clearly a source of strength that we must build upon. Our strategy is to identify gaps, if any, in existing skill sets in different ITES-BPO/KPO verticals and suggest programmes for bridging them through formal and non-formal sectors so that India becomes a leading software developer in the world. Besides, the thrust areas need to be identified where the country has potential to become internationally competitive for achieving significant exports in the field of Electronics hardware manufacturing.

Policy Issues, Programme Reforms & New Initiatives in the Eleventh Plan: Some of the policy issues which need to be addressed in a focused manner in the IT and ITES sector in the country are elaborated here under:

Improving the Supply of Suitable Talent: Our biggest challenge is, of course, in relation to human resources. While we produce a large number of graduates and technologists, the demand of the IT industry is growing and is becoming more discerning. There are problems of quantity and quality in this regard. These problems have to be tackled in different timeframes: the short-term, medium-term and long-term.

In the short term, we need programmes to top up the skill level of graduating students through "finishing schools" and "finishing programmes" which will help resolve the quality problem. As the quality of talent pool is not industry ready, implementation of finishing school concept ensures that the right talent is available for immediate deployment. To enhance the pool of experienced, mid-level managers, that is willing and suitable to work in the IT-ITES sectors, a 'bridge course' could be introduced to equip professionals who may not have read for a course in IT. In the medium term, this kind of training needs to be back-ended into the formal system itself by improving the quality of our technical and general education programmes at the graduate level. This will make graduates far more employable. In the long term, we need to address the quantity problem. The education system needs to be expanded rapidly at all levels. This would also require a huge expansion in our Masters and Doctoral programmes. Easing the supply constraint requires more investment as well as a radical reform of our education system.

There is also a need for starting academic programmes for developing manpower in some of the niche areas like IT in health care, transportation, manufacturing, nanotechnology, animation & entertainment etc. Faculty development is another major issue which needs focus. For this purpose, a National programme on faculty development in niche areas would be required. During the Eleventh Plan period, the above important issues need to be tackled and the government needs to provide the necessary resources and policy framework for achieving the desired objectives. In this national endeavor, industry and government need to work together in close unison. Some of the other measures that need to be introduced in order to maintain and improve the quality of manpower are:

- Introduction of standardized national level tests similar to SAT, GRE, AGRE, MAT etc., for benchmarking of students seeking admissions in undergraduate and postgraduate institutes in India.
- Rating and accreditation of all educational institutions by an independent agency.
- Introduction of a common nation-wide benchmark for assessing graduating students and inclusion of industry needs in this assessment process.
- Making the teaching /academics profession more attractive and respectable.
- Encourage students and working professionals to pursue further education for skill enhancement.
- Periodic review and updation of curriculum to make it more industry oriented and encourage faculty to constantly upgrade skills.

Building Adequate Basic, Business and Social Infrastructure: The growth of IT and ITES industry requires building and strengthening of basic, business and social infrastructure. The incremental infrastructure required to support the projected growth is unlikely to be absorbed into the existing city centres (Tier I/II), which are already witnessing signs of strain. With Tier III/IV cities lacking important elements of business and social infrastructure, decentralized growth of the IT and ITES sector will require a coordinated, large scale (distributed) urban planning exercise. Some of the important initiatives required to be taken include:

- Strengthening of the intra-city road network and public transport infrastructure to decongest existing hubs.
- Decentralization of the industry beyond existing hubs by developing new townships.
- Introduction of faster public transport (high speed trains similar to TGV of France and Bullet of Japan) between important cities.

Ensuring a Favourable Business Policy and Regulatory Environment with Special Focus on Encouraging SMEs and New Ventures: A favourable business policy and a regulatory environment are critical for the success of any sector. The example set by the STPI scheme stands testament to this fact. In order to strengthen India's proposition for sustained leadership in the IT and ITES space, it is essential to actively support the SME sector. In addition, the issue of intellectual property protection, data and information security is a key risk to the sector. Hence, it is essential for India to proactively formulate a robust policy framework to address this challenge. This calls for :(i) Continuation of the Benefits Provided by the STPI Scheme, (ii) Strengthening the IP Protection, Data Privacy and Information Security Environment in the Country, (iii) Providing support for SME Segment Growth to ensure that SMEs can continue to leverage the benefits offered under the STP / SEZ scheme without constraints on where they may be located., and (iv) Ensuring adequate access to venture capital and angel funding for start-ups.

Global Trade Development and Promotion of Global Free Trade in Services: Expansion of the global IT-BPO market opportunity is directly influenced by the policy and regulatory frameworks governing cross-border trade in services. Growth of cross-border trade in services is constrained not only by tariff barriers – but more so by non-tariff barriers (e.g. national treatment in cross-border supply and movement of people). India must continue to work proactively with its trading partners (through the WTO and other trade promotion agencies) to streamline trade in professional services. India must push for the free movement of professionals engaged in delivering services on the basis of formal contracts, through a global GATS or professional services visa. At the same time, it must engage in bilateral or multilateral negotiations on these issues with countries of specific interest to us. Negotiations are also needed to conclude agreements relating to exemption or refund of social security taxes paid by Indian professionals working abroad.

Fostering a Sustainable Ecosystem for Innovation and R&D: In order to structurally strengthen India's proposition and ensure its long-term leadership, it is essential to nurture a sustainable ecosystem for innovation and R&D in the country. This will require a multifaceted approach comprising (a) developing core capabilities at the academic level in identified focus areas; (b) encouraging industry-academia participation in R&D; and (c) facilitating the incubation/commercialization of innovations. IP rights awareness should be increased in institutes and industries. With a view to encourage and reward innovation, there is a need to ensure availability and access to adequate funding for technology entrepreneurs and commercialization of innovation. Research & training should go hand in hand. This is the practice worldwide. The CSIR laboratories should pair with Universities and targeted R&D should be undertaken.

The Transformation of the Industry from BPO to KPO and Related HR Issues: The society is shifting from an era of industrial society into the "knowledge society". Knowledge creation and its applications are primary features of this change in today's networked society. In any industrial society, the growth rate in the services sector is higher than that of the manufacturing sector. Services themselves are also becoming an increasingly integral part of all production businesses and there are relatively more people working in this sector now. This trend is ultimately leading to an increased emphasis on intangible products, which is also called service concepts. Providing services is a much more challenging task than just delivering goods, and, therefore, there will be an increasing focus on making optimal use of resources for maximizing their competitiveness.

The IT and ITES-BPO sector should continuously identify the emerging verticals, which have the potential to grow and generate revenues keeping the dynamic nature of this sector in view. Generating the right kind of manpower with skill-sets requirement for each of the potential vertical is so diverse that it becomes a challenge for the HR function of a company to continuously evolve vertical specific training methodologies and design suitable training modules. Further, the HR companies will have to continuously scan the horizon for the emergence of newer technologies and knowledge areas. The situation will become more complex as the transition from BPO to KPO (Knowledge Process Outsourcing) takes place. Intuitively, one can say that the transition is likely to be very crucial for sustenance of the industry's growth and subsequent establishment in the market place.

It will be essential for each company to build internal capabilities to manage knowledge effectively and also the collective competence building for the Information Technology sector. Managing knowledge is a process which involves multi-period decision framework, starting from investment in research and development to diffusion of knowledge to creation of innovation and ultimately realizing the value through commercialization of innovation and inventions.

Software Technology Parks (STP) Scheme: A favourable business policy and a regulatory environment are critical for the success of any sector and the STP scheme stands testament to this fact. STPs were set up in various parts of the country as per the Resolution issued by the Government in 1993. Over the last few years, it has played a seminal role in placing India on the global map as an IT superpower. In fact, significant credit for the record growth in exports, foreign exchange earnings, employment generation and the development of the Indian IT-ITES sector is attributed to this scheme. Under the STP scheme, units engaged in the export of IT-ITES are entitled to tax benefits under section 10A and 10B of Income Tax Act 1961. However, these benefits under the scheme are scheduled to lapse post assessment year 2009-10.

IT in School Education: Technology could be effectively used for digital delivery of high quality lectures and course material to other institutions and embellish the same with class room teaching for enhancing the learning. ICT tools can make it easier to monitor not only the attendance and performance of the students but also that of the teachers as well. The Management Information Systems (MIS) also need to be developed to monitor the national projects such as Sarva Siksha Abhiyan (SSA), Mid-Day Meal (MDM) and Integrated Child Development Scheme (ICDS) etc.

Gender Empowerment through ICT: The Indian IT-ITeS industry with revenues of US$ 39.6 billion has emerged as the largest private sector employer in the country with direct employment of 1.6 million professionals, and indirect employment for over 6 million people in different sectors. This fast expanding IT and ITeS sector in India has opened new doors of opportunity for women. The participation of women in the IT-BPO workforce is seen as a critical enabling factor for continued growth of the industry. While the percentage of women in the IT-BPO workforce at an entry level is commensurate with their proportion amongst graduating students, anecdotal evidence suggests that this is not so at the middle and senior management positions. However, companies are recognizing that having women on board at all levels in the organization makes good business sense.

IT-BPO companies are, therefore, considering ways to involve and develop women for higher roles and functions.

Their increased professional participation will result in changing the socio-economic status of women within the employing organization and will also contribute towards the breakdown of gender disparity. In a study conducted by Nasscom in 2006, 76 percent of software professionals in IT companies are men, whereas 24 percent are women. However, Nasscom says this ratio is likely to be 65:35 (men: women) by the year 2007. Interestingly, this ratio is reversed in the ITES-BPO sector where the ratio of men to women is 31:69.In line with the basic principles of governance to which the Government is committed under the National Common Minimum Programme, which includes empowerment of women, Government has introduced gender budgeting. In accordance with this Gender Empowerment through ICT should be regular feature during the Eleventh Plan and efforts should be made to support schemes of Gender Empowerment through ICT for reducing Digital Divide.

Faculty Development in IT: The prevailing system of education in India is constrained by several factors. The Government needs to strengthen the education system structurally with a number of strategies. There is a dire need for continuously updating the course content, curriculum and pedagogic methods to make them more relevant to the needs of the industry. Additionally there is a need to take up specific programmes for the development of faculty and provide adequate incentives for making teaching an attractive career option. Some of the policy issues in this regard which need immediate attention are the following:

- Make teaching/academics as attractive a career option as working in the industry. The academic institutes need to provide suitable faculty remuneration as there is a large gap between the salary structures in the industry and in the academics. Industry needs to come forward and supplement the Government efforts through establishment of Chairs for professors, incentives, sponsored research and the like.

- Need to increase the number of faculty positions in the Indian Universities and technical institutions as well as creation of adjunct faculty from industry to address the twin issue of quantity and quality and R&D activities.
- Need to tie up with institutions abroad for professors to come here on sabbatical.
- Need to train the ICT faculty of both the formal and the non-formal sector of education to keep pace with the demands of the industry as well as the technological changes.
- Develop a mechanism to encourage migration of students between formal and non-formal streams to address the issue of quantity. Also introduce a credit system whereby the students can accumulate and carry forward their credits and complete their education at their own pace. This would particularly help the in-service personnel.
- Evolve National Mission for faculty development in general and faculty development in niche ITES areas such as IT in tourism, health, medical and legal services and finance in particular.

IT in Health Sector: The importance of Health in the process of economic and social development and improving the quality of life of our citizens has been well recognized. The Government has identified Health as one of the 7 Thrust Areas and has given focused attention. Since independence, a vast public health infrastructure has been created comprising Public Health Centres (PHCs) and Community Health Centres (CHCs) and District/State and Super Specialty hospitals. In rural areas especially, there are pockets of under-served populations where the vicious circle of poverty, malnutrition and poor health reinforce each other. There is an urgent need to reach out to the un-reached especially in the remote areas. This can effectively be done with the infusion of technology into the health sector.

Integrated disease surveillance projects, creation of district and State Health Data Centres for the surveillance units, networking and operating of district health centres through video based distance communications, early warning system for discase incidence and collection of call centre based information, web-based health management information systems and telemedicine are some of the important areas that need to be operationalized. Electronic health – or e-health is one of the next frontiers of ICT innovations. Some of the well known hospitals in the country have developed Management Information System (MIS) for health which is also known as Medical Information System (MIS), which would go a long way in creation and adoption of nationwide electronic medical records for all patients treated at various hospitals in the country. The issues like data privacy, security and interoperability of systems are to be dealt with properly from an e-health perspective.

IT in Agriculture Sector: Agriculture continues to be one of the mainstays of Indian economy. Increased agricultural production and incomes would put more money in the hands of the people living in the rural areas. Keeping in view the important role that IT can play in boosting productivity and incomes of farmers and reducing the cost of operations, agriculture has been identified as one of the Mission Mode Projects under the National E-Governance Plan (NEGP), a nationwide initiative for promoting e-governance in the country.

By means of IT, the agriculture sector would achieve higher efficiencies to redefine the way in dealing with the production and post harvest losses. The Agricultural Resources Information System is envisaged to create comprehensive database on various parameters related to land use, water use and system for strengthening advisory services to farmers in adopting the latest agricultural production practices. The portal AGMARKNET which provides daily market information on commodity prices in respect of about 300 commodities and 2000 varieties from over 2700 markets is a Sunshine Portal for farmers to bargain better prices for their produce. Similarly, the 'Gyandoot' portal of the State of Madhya Pradesh provides information regarding rates of grains and vegetables, dispenses land records and issues income, domicile and caste certificates. Further attempts need to be made in providing the latest information on real time basis to the farmers and the other rural population in the remotest parts of the country. Market is now the driver for agricultural growth and efficiency of the market depends on effective dissemination of information. IT has the potential to help the agriculture sector to over come some of the traditional barriers to development by improving access to information, expanding the market base, enhancing employment opportunities and making Government services work better. Decision Support System on agricultural production and marketing, water allocation in an irrigation system, and cattle farming system in livestock are required to be developed aggressively.

In the private sector also several initiatives have been taken to optimize the supply chain. 'e-Choupal' has been conceived as a more efficient supply chain aimed at delivering value to its customers around the world on a sustainable basis. The e-Choupal model has been specifically designed to tackle the challenges posed by the unique problems of Indian agriculture, characterized by fragmented farms, weak infrastructure and the involvement of numerous intermediaries, among others.

IT in Rural Sector: Rural Content Providers (RCPs): The creation of local/rural content is of utmost importance in order to make the PCs and internet an attractive proposition to a much larger number of people. Involving the private sector in this regard would also be essential. Therefore, it is felt that a new entrepreneurial category of Rural Content Providers (RCPs) would give a further boost to and drive the demand, both for PCs and Internet access as well as for rural connectivity. It will also help in better utilization of the cable/ wireless network already laid, or being planned in the rural areas by the bandwidth providers. The Rural Content Providers would provide content and other facilities, including entertainment, which will be of interest to the rural population.

Content creation would be a specialized area requiring thorough understanding of the local requirements and language which can only be done through local entrepreneurs. The business model of such an RCP would vary from region to region and would be driven by the market. The Department of IT and the Department of Telecommunications need to evolve a suitable strategy to encourage such RCPs. Information Technology revolution would remain incomplete unless the benefit of this revolution reaches rural masses.

The Path Ahead: The outlook for Indian IT/ITESBPO remains bright and the sector is poised to achieve its target of US$ 86.6 billion in export revenues by FY 2011-12. In order to achieve these targets, both the Government of India as well as the industry needs to work in unison. While the basic policy framework and fiscal incentives as enumerated above need to be put in place by the Government, the industry associations and the industries need to actively support the initiatives.

FINANCIAL SERVICES

Introduction: The financial services sector in the country has been displaying a varying growth rate in the recent past. The financial sector as a whole is estimated to employ between 3.5-4.0 million people, including direct employees and agency forces. To support the GDP growth aspiration of 9-10%, the financial sector would need to grow by 25-30% annually over the next five years. Financial sector penetration in India remains low relative to many markets, with bank credit/ GDP at under 50.0%, overall insurance premium/ GDP at under 5.0% and general insurance premium/ GDP at under 1.0%. The underlying GDP growth and higher penetration potential offer strong growth opportunities for the financial sector. The financial sector also has substantial potential for employment creation.

This sector performs the vital functions of enabling

productivity and income growth in the economy as a whole, and has an equally important part to play in making this growth more inclusive. The sector has to be enabled to attain an increasing level of sophistication so as to meet the requirements of globalizing trade and industry and the increasing engagement of the Indian economy with the rest of the world, both on the current as well as on the capital accounts. The government has recently received the report of the Expert Committee on making Mumbai an International Financial Centre. This report has made very far reaching recommendations on fiscal and monetary policies, financial sector regulation and supervision as well as on the development of various financial markets. While these recommendations would be relevant to the needs of medium and large scale industry and commerce, it would be necessary to look at certain further policy measures in order to ensure that small and marginal farmers, micro enterprises in the unorganized sector, the weaker and disadvantaged sections of society and the relatively backward regions and States are enabled to participate more fully in the growth process.

Financial Inclusion: Financial Inclusion can be described as the delivery of banking and other financial services at affordable costs to the vast sections of disadvantaged and low-income groups. To bring the 'financially excluded' population within the formal financial system, many policy initiatives have been taken, such as making available a basic banking 'no frills' account either with 'nil' or very low minimum balances, issuing of General Credit Cards to eligible beneficiaries without insistence on security, purpose or end use of credit, introduction of Kisan Credit Cards, allowing banks to utilize the services of Non-Governmental Organizations, Self Help Groups, Micro Finance Institutions and other Civil Society Organization as intermediaries in providing financial services, credit linking of Self Help Groups, Support to MFIs and introduction of Financial Sector (Regulation and Development) Bill, 2007 to develop and regulate the MFIs and constitution of Financial Inclusion Fund and Financial Inclusion Technology Fund of Rs.500 crore each to strengthen the institutional and technological infrastructure for greater financial inclusion. We have to introduce suitable policy interventions and technological innovations to maximize financial inclusion during the Eleventh Plan period.

Extent and Causes of Financial Exclusion: Lack of access to financial services such as credit, savings, and insurance at an affordable cost not only results in exclusion but also acts as a constraint to growth impetus in the rural and unorganized sectors. Despite years of policies aimed at financial inclusion, a large number of households do not have access to formal financial services even today.

Financial exclusion covers exclusion from any or all of the financial services necessary for participating in a modern market economy. Nevertheless, exclusion from credit provision has been looked at as being more significant than that from other services. There is a rural-urban divide and a regional skew to financial exclusion.

The NSSO Situation Assessment Survey on "Indebtedness of Farmer Households" (2003) reveals that 51.4% of farmer households do not access credit either from formal or non-formal sources.

There are several reasons for financial exclusion. Lack of awareness, low income/assets, social exclusion and illiteracy are demand side factors. On the supply side, distance from branches, branch timings, cumbersome documentation and procedures, unsuitable products, language and staff attitudes are reasons for exclusion.

While steps need to be taken to improve the access to and the supply of credit and other financial services, there can be no overemphasis of the importance of building up the capacity of the weaker sections to use financial services. To some extent, a financial service such as insurance would be necessary to use another financial service such as credit, financial literacy would help in using savings, credit and insurance services etc., but there remain several other very important factors outside of the financial sector that are complementary to financial services and need to considered as integrated package.

On the supply side, the post 1991 period has also seen significant changes in the credit provision for the weaker sections. Despite emphasis on increasing the credit penetration and outreach of institutional sources of credit, the number of rural bank branches has declined from 35,134 in March 1991 to 30,572 in March 2006. Even the number of small borrowers accounts (less than Rs.25, 000) has declined from 625.48 lakh to 387.33 lakh. The result has been that the share of money lenders in the total dues of rural house-holds has increased from 17.5% in 1991 to 29.6% in 2002.(All India Debt and Investment Survey as on June 30, 2002 NSS 59th Round Released in December 2005)

A continuing policy measure is the stipulation of priority sector lending. However, this has got diluted in the last 10 years by shift in focus to better creditworthy activities like, housing, transport, professional activities, etc.

The Priority Sector now comprises agriculture (both direct and indirect), small scale industries, small road and water transport operators, small business, retail trade, professional and self-employed persons, State sponsored organizations for SC/ST, education, housing loans, micro credit, loans to software, and food and agro processing sector.

The share of agriculture in total bank credit declined sharply from 15.9% at end-March 1990 to 9.6% by end-March 2001. During this period, however, the share of agriculture in GDP also declined significantly. As a result, the credit intensity of the agriculture sector (credit to agriculture sector as percentage of sectoral GDP) remained broadly at the same level. Credit to agriculture picked up significantly from 2004-05 onwards. The Government announced on 18th June, 2004 a package for doubling the flow of credit to agriculture and allied activities in a period of three years commencing from

2004-05 over the amount disbursed during the year 2003-04.

The credit intensity of the sector increased sharply from 11.1% in 2001-02 to 27% in 2005-06. The number of borrowal accounts in the agriculture sector also increased from 19.84 million in 2000-01 to 26.66 million in 2004-05. Within the overall minimum priority sector target of 40% of net bank credit (NBC), the share of agriculture is 18 %. The share of agricultural loans as percentage of NBC for public sector banks was 15.3% at end-March 2005 and 15.2% at end March 2006. Private Sector banks were at 13.5% both as at end-March 2005 and 2006. While commercial banks have taken care of the needs of small farmers, they have not done so in respect of marginal/sub-marginal farmers, tenants/share croppers, oral lessees, non-cultivator households etc.

Distribution of credit up to Rs. 2 lakh by Scheduled Commercial Banks (SCBs) over the last ten years reveals a disturbing trend. Number of loan accounts for availing credit up to Rs 25000, has declined from 5.19 crore in 1996 to 3.84 crore in 2006. As a proportion of total loan accounts, it has declined from 91.6% to 45% during the same period. Similarly, the outstanding credit has reduced drastically from about 14.2% of total bank credit in 1996 to 3% in 2006. However, the average outstanding has increased from Rs. 6985 to Rs. 11769.

For credit disbursed above Rs. 25000 and up to Rs. 2 lakh, number of loan accounts has increased nearly ten fold and credit outstanding has multiplied over seven times. Consequently, the average loan outstanding has declined from about Rs. 70,000 in 1996 to Rs 52,500 in 2006.

Disbursal of credit displays the rural-urban divide. Rural and semi-urban loan accounts, as a proportion of total loan accounts, have declined from about 79% in 1996 to about 59 % in 2006. The fall has been sharper in the rural segment. The credit outstanding in this category has declined by about 5 percentage points from 29.64% of bank credit to 24.72% during the same period. On the contrary, the urban and metro segments reflect the opposite trend. Number of loan accounts in urban and metro areas has multiplied about two and four times, respectively. As a proportion of total loan accounts, it increased from about 21% in 1996 to about 41 % in 2006. The loan outstanding has increased by about 5 percentage points from 70% in 1996 to 75% in 2006.

Artisan, Village and Tiny industries and other small scale industries (AVT & other SSIs) have received insufficient credit. Number of AVT & other SSIs loan accounts, as percentage of total bank accounts has declined by 4.6 percentage points from 7.2% in 1996 to 2.6% in 2006. In absolute terms, it declined from 40.9 lakh to 21.8 lakh. Loan accounts have declined secularly during the period in rural, semi-urban and urban areas. However, in metro it has increased. The outstanding credit has also declined by 6.6 percentage points from 10.7% of bank credit in 1996 to 4.1% in 2006. The decline across rural and urban areas is, however more pronounced in the metros. Though the loan accounts during the period have nearly halved, the average outstanding credit has increased more than four fold from Rs 66,750 in 1996 to Rs. 2, 85,500 in 2006. While artisan, village and tiny industries are concentrated predominantly in rural areas, other SSIs are dominant in the urban and metros This reflects that the artisan, village and tiny industries which is relatively less credit worthy have been credit starved..

The share of credit to SSIs has declined from 15% of NBC in 1998 to 6.4% in 2005-06. Including small business, retail trade etc., the total share is less than 10% of NBC. Housing has gone up from 2.9% to 9.23%.

Self Help Groups (SHGs) and their linking up to the banking system has been a very notable feature of the provision of financial services to the weaker sections in recent years. However, apart from the fact that this has been largely in the south, the overall quantum of credit extended is still quite small. As at end-March 2006, 22.39 lakh SHGs were linked to banks. Cumulative lending amounted to Rs.11398 crore. The current outstanding credit is around Rs 4000 crore which is a very small fraction of NBC. About 24 million families have been assisted. The average bank loan per SHG has increased from Rs. 18,227 in 2001 to Rs. 32,012 in 2005.

Policy Issues: A number of committees have provided guidance on improving financial inclusion. The Sub-Group on Financial Services headed by Shri K.V.Kamath (2007) is the most recent one. The C. Rangarajan Committee on Financial Inclusion (2007) has, in its Interim Report, made detailed recommendations on supply side solutions to improve the delivery of financial services through traditional and non-conventional channels. It has also laid emphasis on complementary demand side measures that are necessary. The Vaidyanathan Committee on restructuring of cooperatives (2004) and the Committee on Moneylender Legislation (2006) have recommended policy measures to improve financial inclusion.

Some of the key policy issues emerging out of these and other reports for extending the outreach and depth of financial inclusion are discussed in the succeeding paragraphs.

Interest Rate Caps: Interest rates on loans made by banks have been deregulated from 1994, with the exception of export credit and loans up to Rs 2 lakh. In the latter case, the interest rate cannot exceed the bank's notified benchmark PLR. Recently, the Government has announced a subsidy of 2% to banks for extending production credit up to Rs 3 lakh for agriculture at 7%. However, as the Report on Currency and Finance 2005-06 states "although the supply-led approach to rural credit prior to the 1990s ensured availability of credit at a subsidized rate, it turned out to be financially unsustainable as it impacted on the health of credit institutions adversely".

The entire issue of deregulating/regulating the interest rate is embedded in the question of whether access and timely availability of credit should be an overriding concern rather than the cost of credit per se.

The Working Group on Outreach of Institutional Finance

and Cooperative Reforms examined this issue and also conducted studies, through its sub groups on the actual costs incurred in financing small borrowers in the rural areas. A sample study of lending by a public sector bank showed that the all inclusive cost of loans of Rs 25000 and less is 21 %. In the case of a private sector bank, it was found that the cost of direct lending was much more than when the lending was through an intermediary MFI. However, the cost difference declines as the size of the loans increases. The all inclusive cost, as per this study, works out to as much as 33.1% for direct lending of loan of Rs.10,000 while this is 17.5% for a loan of Rs.25,000 through an MFI. The overall balance sheet analysis of RRBs and CCBs produced a cost of 7.75% on earning assets for RRBs and 10.16% for CCBs. Commercial banks estimates range from 7.5% to 13.5%. A College of Agricultural Banking study of 22 MFIs showed an average cost of 30.2%.

There is clearly a need for carrying out periodic studies based on scientifically selected samples and factoring in all costs to arrive at the actual cost of lending to small borrowers in rural areas.

In addition to the interest rates charged borrowers have to incur other costs, such as submitting certificates/documents (land documents, search reports by lawyers, 'no dues' certificate from other bank branches, valuation certificates, etc.) and often bribes. Taking all these into account, the total cost of borrowing through formal institutional channels may not be less than the rates charged by formal credit channels.

If documentation and other procedures are simplified, thereby reducing the transaction costs of farmers significantly, farmers may not mind paying market driven rates of interests, covering the costs of funds, transaction costs and risk costs of the banks. Allowing interest rates to be market driven and taking into account the risk perceptions of the banks, would lead to the banks considering agricultural lending as a viable business proposition.

The Report on Currency and Finance itself quotes the Prime Minister to raise what are significant questions relating to credit to the weaker sections. It raises the fundamental issue of whether farmers need reliable access to credit at reasonable rates or a lower rate of interest, whether we need to create new institutional structures etc.

There appears to exist an element of inconsistency in the stipulations relating to interest rates. While the interest rate on direct lending by banks up to a limit of Rs 2 lakh cannot be at a rate higher than the Bank's PLR, there is no such restriction if the lending is to an ultimate borrower through the intermediation of an MFI. The Reserve Bank of India in 2000 deregulated the interest rates on loans made by commercial banks to MFIs, and interest rates on loans made by MFIs to borrowers. Micro-credit extended by commercial banks either directly or through an intermediary was to be considered as part of a bank's priority sector lending. Again in 2006, RBI emphasized that the interest rates applicable to loans given by banks to MFIs or by MFIs to SHGs/member beneficiary would be left to their discretion. This leads to an anomalous situation where loans to the same beneficiaries if dispensed through alternate channels of financing are priced differently. In order to remove this anomaly, no interest rate ceilings should be imposed on the banks by the Government.

Data shows that around 82% of the lending by banks is taking place at sub-PLR rates. While better creditworthy corporates are getting credit at sub -PLR rates, the agriculture and SSI sectors and others are charged PLR or even higher rates. This would again point out to the need to carry out proper costing studies for credit provision to different classes of customers. It must be recognized that if the effort for financial inclusion of the underprivileged is to be sustained, the cost of providing such services should invariably be met. However, the model should, at the same time, penalise inefficiencies in providing credit. Therefore, costs should be appropriately benchmarked in accordance with best practices.

A free interest rate regime and competition should be recognized as the primary means of ensuring reasonable rates; this should be supplemented by the publication of the results of such studies.

It is necessary to recognize that there are limitations beyond which the institutional credit system will not be able to provide services in spite of the adoption of technology, especially when it pertains to disadvantaged groups. Experience through case studies shows that expansion of micro finance has helped in smoothening the interest rates charged by the informal sector.

While the approach of RBI has been very open and driven by the larger interest for the development of the micro-finance sector, there have been instances of the State Governments regulating the interest rate. State Governments have taken the plea that MFIs charge usurious rates of interest and this increases the indebtedness of the usually poor borrowers.

Consultative Group to Assist the Poor (CGAP) guiding principles on regulation and supervision of micro-finance state that interest rates caps, where they are in force, almost always hurt the poor by limiting services far more than they help the poor by lowering rates. The Report of the Internal Group to Examine Issues relating to Rural Credit and Micro Finance (Khan Committee) of RBI has also deliberated on this issue. The Report mentions that the empirical data in respect of several micro-finance projects being carried out in different parts of the world prove that timely availability and right quantity of credit, and not the interest rate, is crucial to the success of micro finance programmes. Since the method of costing applied by micro finance institutions is fundamentally different from that followed by banks, the methodology for applying interest rates for them would be different from banks. Since providing services at the doorstep of the customer has a cost, no undue intervention is required to set the interest rates charged to the ultimate borrower through the financial intermediation route. This is best left to the commercial judgment of the borrowing MFIs and lending institutions.

It has been argued that both Central and State Governments can play a central role in reducing interest rates without introducing rate caps. This can be done by creating a database and monitoring system for interest rates being charged by MFIs. Under the system, it would be mandatory for MFIs to report the effective interest rate offerings periodically. However, transparency in fixation of interest rates is the major bottleneck. At present, there is no uniform agreed methodology followed by MFIs for disclosing effective interest rate charged including loan processing fees, bad debt provisions and other ancillary charges. This makes it difficult to compare interest rates across MFIs. One of the options could be self-regulation i.e. associations of MFIs themselves voluntarily adopt and enforce a code of conduct including disclosure norms. As self-regulatory organizations have serious limitations to enforce their rules, the other option is formal regulation of the sector. This would include formulation and enforcement of uniform financial reporting guidelines including norms for treatment of non performing assets; unambiguous interest rate disclosure guidelines including norms for disclosing loan processing fees, bad debt provisions and other hidden charges; clear conduct codes for behaviour of MFI staff with penalty for breach of conduct rules; and audit provision for MFIs above a certain level of portfolio.

Ratings of MFIs by external agencies such as SIDBI could also be thought of to promote transparency in the operations of MFIs.

With the use of IT solutions and transparency in pricing coupled with growing competition amongst MFIs, it is expected that interest rate charged by MFIs would come down. Credit dispensation through alternate channels, namely, MFIs, SHGs, NBFCs, Housing Finance companies, Post Offices would be effective in increasing access, reducing transaction costs as also in improving recovery.

Modes of Extending Outreach:

Up-scaling SHGs-Bank Linkage Programme (SBLP): Essentially, two forms of providing micro-credit are being followed i.e SBLP and MFIs. Within SHG-bank linkage model, SHGs are formed by NGOs/SHPIs and credit is extended by banks to SHGs directly. This is the predominant form of disbursement of credit within the SBLP model.

The geographical distribution of both SHGs-bank linkage and MFIs is highly skewed. The Southern States account for the bulk of the SHGs. However, in recent years, SBLP has been making inroads into regions with large percentage of rural poor. About 90% of the SHGs that are linked to banks are of women.

SBLP has registered an impressive growth during the last five to seven years. At present, 90% of the micro-credit is being disbursed through the SHGs-bank linkage model. The SHGs linked to banks has increased from 2.64 lakh in 2000-01 to 22.39 lakh in 2005-06. Despite such an impressive growth, a vast gap between the demand and supply of micro-credit exists. As per the estimate by the Task Force headed by V.S. Vyas (2007), the minimum requirement of micro credit is Rs.70000 crore as against the supply of Rs. 11378 crore. This programme is also concentrated in the southern states. However, in 2005, NABARD has identified 13 priority states accounting for the bulk of India's poor for special efforts and location specific strategies.

Under the SBLP, the average loan per member is less than Rs. 4000. This is grossly insufficient for financing income generating activities. The interest rate charged to members has been reported to be 15 to 24 per cent per annum. The cost of forming and nurturing the group up to the stage of credit linkage is borne by NABARD. Ministry of Rural Development norms provide for Rs. 10000 per group as the cost of formation of groups.

The binding constraint in the SBLP is the ability to form groups and to build up their capacities. This, in turn, is strongly dependent on the availability of committed NGOs and SHG Promoting Institutions (SHPIs). The Rangarajan Committee has identified the SBLP as one of the two main instruments for achieving financial inclusion and has suggested that the Departments of Women and Child Development should be actively involved in this process. Upon the recommendation of this Committee, a Financial Inclusion Fund has been set up by NABARD for promotional activities. NABARD is already engaged in a variety of capacity building efforts in this area. NABARD's programme needs to be more closely integrated with those of State governments, specially in the 13 priority states. It is to be noted that the National Commission for Enterprises in the Unorganized Sector (NCEUS) has also made a similar recommendation for a fund to be used for promotional activities.

At the same time, it has been suggested by some that this model may be allowed to grow organically in response to needs and capabilities and there should be emphasis on quality rather than quantity. SHGs should not be allowed to go the cooperatives way. Cooperatives were burdened with non-credit business i.e. used as a mechanism to deliver government programme such as PDS, sale of fertilizer etc. They subsequently became politicized. SHGs being such a large scale movement are also susceptible to politicization. It needs to be ensured that SHGs retains their character as a peoples' movement and do not become a tool in power politics.

Interestingly, the Vaidyanathan Committee states that cooperatives, of the mutual thrift and credit type, are the only form of organization by which economically disadvantaged individuals and groups, through voluntary collective action, overcome their disadvantageous position in an unequal market and promote their well being. It further adds that credit will be put to good use in organizations in which members know each other first hand, are closely linked through kinship and social relations, and have a strong mutual stake in the proper use of the common credit pool. One would not be mistaken if this description were understood as being one of SHGs. In fact, there is nothing new in the SHG concept that has not been embedded in that of the cooperatives earlier. That the cooperatives have reached their present state should serve as a serious warning to the SHG movement as well.

The MFI Sector: In the MFI model, the MFIs both form the groups and provide credit to SHGs/individuals. MFIs raise funds from banks and financial institutions for on-lending to SHGs and individuals.

MFIs are an amorphous collection of legal entities, both for-profit and not-for-profit institutions. Amongst not-for-profit institutions are included NGOs incorporated as trusts/societies, cooperatives set up under the Cooperative Acts and Section 25 companies under the Companies Act. For-profit MFIs include NBFCs incorporated under the Companies Act and regulated by the RBI.

In the MFI model, the rate of interest charged is higher (at about 20 to 24%) than the SBLP model as MFIs have to charge a rate of interest that recovers cost of funds as well as the cost of formation of groups. Sa-Dhan's voluntary code of conduct lays down that MFIs will charge reasonable rate of interest i.e. 21 to 24 per cent per annum. This is comparable to the rate of interest charged by SHGs from their members. Even the cost of formation and nurturing the groups is borne by the MFIs themselves. Cost of funds to MFIs is higher than the rate at which banks lend to SHGs under SBLP. Transaction costs are also higher owing to weekly collections and delivery of services at the doorstep. On the flip side, transparency in fixation of rate of interest and disclosure norms, consumer protection and coercive practices of MFIs have emerged as the major concerns.

MFIs require funds for credit expansion and on lending to SHGs/individual members. As of now, studies reveal that Indian MFIs are very highly leveraged compared to the rest of the world. With a low equity base, the ability of MFIs to raise debt resources from banks and other financial institutions is limited. Several measures to enlarge equity capital of MFIs include relaxing the constraint on equity investment by venture capital into MFIs, lowering the minimum capital requirement for foreign equity participation and enhancing the corpus of equity support from NABARD.

Revitalization of cooperatives: Cooperatives have the largest nominal outreach amongst the rural financial institutions including commercial banks. Presently, they are at a crossroads owing to resource constraints, poor governance, bad management and inefficiency. Based on the recommendations of the Vaidyanathan Committee Government of India has formulated a revival package for restructuring and strengthening of the rural cooperative credit institutions. Seventeen States have accepted 'in-principle' the revised revival package as formulated by the Government of India. Of the seventeen, twelve States have executed Memorandum of Understanding (MoU) with GOI and NABARD. The conditionalities free the societies from the necessity of being part of the three tier structure. Individual societies are also to be free to establish business contact with commercial banks and borrow from any RBI regulated institution.. Freedom from compulsory federation would help in reducing unnecessary tiers in financing that add to costs. They are also to be free to decide interest rates on deposits and advances subject to RBI regulations. These reforms are salutary and will enable the cooperatives to function on sound commercial lines. The insistence on signing the MoU with its conditionalities, and acceptance of guidelines prescribed by RBI for ensuring 'fit and proper' criteria for Directors in the Boards and CEOs of rural cooperatives are apparently some of the reasons for slow pace of implementation of the revival package.

It is imperative that the revival package is implemented in toto without diluting the contingent legal, financial, regulatory and institutional reforms. This would have the effect of cleansing the balance sheets and strengthening the capital base of rural cooperatives so that they begin on a clean slate and are at par with other rural financial institutions. However, there are several valid concerns that need to be addressed so that the financial and institutional sustainability of the rural cooperatives is not impaired.

The Vaidyanathan Committee states that, cooperative societies in India, unlike the world over, have not been mutual, but only agencies for credit dispensation. Upper tiers were created to provide refinance for the lower. This resulted in a structure driven by borrowers at all levels. The Committee therefore recommended that there should be an aggressive effort to convert pure credit to thrift-cum-credit societies. In this form, it is expected that there would be natural incentives for good governance. This vision has been largely preserved in the reform package that has now been worked out. However, the process of organic growth that this entails is likely to constrain the ability of the cooperatives to quickly scale up their operations.

The Vaidyanathan Committee has recommended liquidation of the non-viable and defunct PACs. The exact modality of liquidation however, has not been spelt out. As the number of PACs to be liquidated is quite large, transitional arrangements need to be put in place to maintain the ground level credit flow. Mergers with healthy PACs or take-over by neighbouring PACs may adversely affect the financial performance and burden the functioning of the taking-over PACs. A better solution lies in development of new PACs under the Model Act suggested by the Vaidyanathan Committee. However, this would be a time-taking but a sustainable option in the long-run.

Cooperatives offer high rates of interest on deposits. Cooperatives also suffer from high transaction costs owing to overstaffing and salaries unrelated to the magnitude of business. High risk costs arise on account of low recovery levels, lack of adequate risk mitigation systems and procedures, absence of appropriate credit appraisal and monitoring, and over exposure to agricultural lending. Actual repayments are influenced by ad-hoc Government decisions to suspend, delay or even waive recovery. The revival package, significantly, does not disempower the state governments from giving directives to the credit cooperatives. These powers have been used often in the past to subject the cooperatives to commercially unsound decisions. Costs of funds are also high as PACs depend on borrowings from upper tier cooperatives. Lack of information about credit worthiness of the clients further compounds the problem. The lending rates need to cover cost of funds, transaction costs and risk costs. While the Vaidyanathan Committee has identified these factors that increase the cost of cooperative credit operations, it has not adequately suggested mechanisms to reduce the associated transactions and risk costs.

The apprehension, therefore, is that the implementation of the revival package is unlikely to provide any substantial remedy to the problem of financial exclusion. This would be even truer of the production and investment financing needs of agriculture. There appears to be no alternative to a vigorous increase in the outreach and the scale of rural operations of the commercial banks.

Scheduled Commercial Banks (SCBs)/Regional Rural Banks (RRBs): While the rural branch network of commercial banks had steadily grown in the years following nationalisation in 1969, there has been a rollback since 1991. The average rural population served by a bank branch has therefore gone up, as shown by the following numbers.

However, there is an opinion that the existing rural branch infrastructure can be more intensively used so as to service a much larger customer base. A major recommendation of the Rangarajan Committee is that banks be given targets to add at least 250 farmer accounts per year per branch. This, the Committee feels, will enable covering all the unbanked farmer households in the next five years. Prescribing a target based approach for commercial banks to extend their out reach in rural areas may not be a viable option until and unless banks are allowed to charge rate of interest that covers their cost of funds, transaction costs and risk costs.

While several policy measures have been initiated to augment the credit flow to small and marginal borrowers, the results speak differently. During 1996 and 2006, the loan outstanding for accounts up to Rs 2 lakh credit has declined from 25.3% to 16.4 % of bank credit. These loans are disbursed at or below PLR. Sub-PLR lending has increased from 39% in Sep. 2004 to 82 % in March 2007. These loans are essentially disbursed to better creditworthy corporates. However, agriculture and SSI sectors in particular, AVT & other SSIs whose loan outstanding is more than Rs. 2 lakh are charged interest rates above PLR. This has several implications. Lending at below PLR lacks transparency and affects both lenders and borrowers. Secondly, to compensate for sub-PLR lending, other segments are charged higher rates of interest thus leading to cross-subsidisation of the economically well-off borrowers by the economically poor borrowers.

The employment intensive and greater regional spread of AVT & other SSIs make them an engine of inclusive growth. However, they are considered more risky by the banks and collaterals are insisted upon. This has been partly addressed by setting up of a Credit Guarantee Fund Trust for SSIs. This fund guarantees up to 75% of the credit risk subject to loan cap of Rs. 50 lakh per borrower. The other option to obviate the need for collateral could be introducing independent rating of borrowers and generating their credit history.

Today's small entrepreneur is tomorrow's big businessman, if provided appropriate financial support. Banks have to be proactive and gear up their risk assessment and management capacities. They have to finance the first time entrepreneurs, notwithstanding the risk, if financial inclusion is to become a reality. The inevitability of some degree of failed ventures should not lead to unreasonable attachment of accountability which otherwise leads to risk aversion amongst lenders. Prudential norms need to be laid down by the regulator to provide this comfort.

Along with the above, it may be necessary to modify the priority sector lending guidelines by creating sub limits for lending to the weaker sections. As suggested by the National Commission for Enterprises in the Unorganized Sector, a sub target of 10 % should be reserved for marginal and small farmers within the 18 % reserved for agriculture. The flow of credit against this sub-target should be separately monitored. Similarly, a separate target of 10 % for small and micro enterprises, of which again 4 % is reserved for micro enterprises with a capital investment of less than Rs 5 lakh, should be imposed and enforced. Along with the freeing of interest rates that has been recommended above, this would help in credit reaching the needy sections.

There have been some suggestions made that the priority sector targets should be enforced in a different fashion than hitherto. A suggestion that merits consideration is that the targets be made tradeable amongst banks. This would have the merit of acting as means of achieving the targets at the lowest possible cost.

A major step taken recently is to permit banks to extend their outreach through engaging Business Facilitators (BF) and Business Correspondents (BC). Banks are required to formulate their own schemes in line with the guidelines of the RBI to operationalise these mechanisms. Though these guidelines were brought out more than one and a half years ago, the NCEUS notes that banks are not inclined to adopt this model because of cost considerations. They therefore suggest that some incentives may be provided to banks, in the form of tax or other benefits, to adopt this model. The Rangarajan Committee says that the banking system has not yet been able to fully appreciate the business gains that could accrue from adopting the model. It adds that discussions with a cross section of bankers reveals that the muted response is, in part, due to disinclination on the part of the banks to absorb the costs involved on grounds of its impact on the viability of operations.

Prohibition on banks to charge more than the PLR on loans less than Rs 2 lakh has made the BC model unworkable for provision of micro-credit. Even if the banks were willing to absorb the difference between their PLR and their cost of funds, margins would not be adequate to compensate the BCs to cover the costs of originating, monitoring and collecting loans.. Second, under the model, the bank is responsible for omissions and commissions of the BC. Third, the lack of IT connectivity (owing to cost considerations) would make it difficult to report and incorporate the BC's transactions in the books of the bank by the end of the next working day. For these reasons BC model has received a rather lukewarm response from the banks. However, this seems to be the best available option for increasing financial inclusion. Apart from removing interest rate controls, a systematic programme for capacity building for the BCs, establishing robust procedures for monitoring their performance and rating them, and the building up of IT connectivity, perhaps even by sharing it amongst banks so as to reduce costs, are all essential for this model to succeed.

The industry feels that financial sector participants would find it difficult to expand into underserved areas in the absence of appropriate payment processing infrastructure. More than 80% of India's financial transactions are processed in physical cash. Cash as means of payment has a large cost in terms of handling, transaction processing, holding and risk of loss. Looking ahead, card-based solutions are likely to emerge as the key mechanism for delivering financial services to the unbanked. There is therefore a need to create a national payments system with participation by all banks, reduce transaction costs and substantially increase the deployment for POS terminals and their utilization for both high and small value payments.

India has achieved good mobile penetration both geographically and in terms of socio-economic classes. The total number of mobile phone connections has already greatly exceeded the number of bank accounts. South Africa has reportedly pioneered the large scale use of mobiles for payment. Japan, South Korea and other countries also are said to be using this method. Enabling mobile payments would facilitate cheaper payment processing, wide geographic coverage, online payments with straight through processing and financial inclusion. The mobile phone can be used as a device to transfer funds and make payments from a bank account using appropriate authentication protocols.

Traditional Moneylenders: The All India Debt and Investment Survey (NSS Fifty ninth Round) has revealed that share of institutional agencies in the total cash dues of urban households had increased from 72% in 1991 to 75.1% in 2002 and that of moneylenders had also increased during the period from 10.2% to 14.1%. In the case of rural households on the other hand, the share of institutional agencies had in fact declined from 64% in 1991 to 57.1% in 2002. And more significantly, the share of moneylenders had increased in the same period from 17.5% to 29.6% in the case of rural households.

Despite measures to extend institutional credit especially in rural areas, the dependence on moneylenders has only increased. Thus there is a case to look at the possibility of using moneylenders for providing credit within a regulated framework. Usurious rates of interest and coercive practices are a reality that needs to be appropriately addressed.

International experience also suggests that moneylenders perform similar activities all over the world both in developed and developing countries. Internationally, the nature of money lending laws is regulatory. The emphasis of such laws is on protecting the interests of the borrowers by capping the rate of interest and curbing coercive recovery practices.

The Technical group of the RBI to review legislations on money lending in its report has also recommended that registration of money lenders should be made compulsory and penalty imposed on those conducting business without registration. It has also recommended that the State Government should stipulate the maximum rate of interest that could be charged by the money lenders. The group has also recommended a model legislation for adoption by the State Government to regulate money lenders The legislation provides incentives for registration and mainstreaming activity of money lending. It also provides for penalties for violation of its provisions as well as disincentives to those who circumvent the law in the form of more stringent action against unregistered lenders.

A major issue that needs to be resolved here is the regulatory capacity of state governments, who are the competent authorities for this purpose. A possible solution could be to outsource the regulatory function to the banking system. The incentive of obtaining credit from banks to enlarge their businesses could be used to overcome the fear of costs associated with registration. Government could consider mainstreaming money lending by instituting an effective regulatory framework as has been done worldwide.

Building up the Demand Side: Perhaps the greatest benefits of public policy initiatives towards financial inclusion are in the area of creating systemic infrastructure for provision of credit and other financial services. Specific measures include creating credit registries, national identification numbers, payment systems, electronic commodity and auction markets and weather measurement systems – all of which are public goods which would help stimulate economic activity. Other measures that would help generate demand for financial services include public investment in rural infrastructure programs, vocational training programs, and measures to improve market linkages that help micro entrepreneurs find reliable channels for marketing their products and services.

New Initiatives: There are certain Non-Governmental Organisations, Societies, Trusts and Cooperative Societies operating in the micro financial sector that are engaged in providing credit and other financial services to the economically active low income people especially women, poor households and their micro enterprises. However, the financial activities undertaken by such organizations lack a formal statutory framework. It was, therefore, considered expedient to provide a formal statutory framework for the promotion, development and orderly growth of the Micro Credit Sector. Accordingly, the Micro Financial Sector (Development and Regulation) Bill, 2007 was introduced in the Lok Sabha on 20.3.2007. Some of the important features of the Bill are given below:

- entrust the function of development and regulation of the micro financial sector to the National Bank for Agricultural and Rural Development (National Bank);
- define various entities engaged in the activity of micro finance such as cooperative societies, mutual benefit societies or mutually aided societies registered under any State enactments or multi-State co-operative societies registered under the Multi-State Cooperative Societies Act, 2002, societies registered under the Societies Registration Act, 1860 or any other State enactments governing such societies and a trust created under the Indian Trust Act, 1882 or public trust registered under any State enactments, that will be governed by the regulatory framework proposed to be set up;
- define various categories of beneficiaries of micro financial services as eligible clients including Self Help Groups (SHGs) or joint liability groups of such eligible clients;
- provide for extending micro financial services to eligible clients by way of financial assistance subject to ceilings to be prescribed and such other financial services as may be specified by the National Bank;

- provide for constitution of Micro Finance Development Council to advise the National Bank on formulation on policies, schemes, and other measures required in the interest of orderly growth and development of the micro finance sector; and
- provide for constitution of Micro Finance Development and Equity Fund to be utilized for the development of micro finance sector.

The Bill is currently under examination with the Standing Committee on Finance.

Index